Bringing Jesus into My World

RELATIONSHIPS

By Ralph Ennis, Rebecca Goldstone, Judy Gomoll, Dennis Stokes, Christine Weddle

NavPress is the publishing ministry of The Navigators, an international Christian organization and leader in personal spiritual development. NavPress is committed to helping people grow spiritually and enjoy lives of meaning and hope through personal and group resources that are biblically rooted, culturally relevant, and highly practical.

For a free catalog go to www.NavPress.com or call 1.800.366.7788 in the United States or 1.800.839.4769 in Canada.

© 2008 by The Navigators

All rights reserved. No part of this publication may be reproduced in any form without written permission from NavPress, P.O. Box 35001, Colorado Springs, CO 80935. www.navpress.com

NAVPRESS and the NAVPRESS logo are registered trademarks of NavPress. Absence of ® in connection with marks of NavPress or other parties does not indicate an absence of registration of those marks.

ISBN-13: 978-1-60006-261-2
ISBN-10: 1-60006-261-X

Cover design by The DesignWorks Group, Jason Gabbert, www.thedesignworksgroup.com

Content Development Team: Ralph Ennis, Judy Gomoll, Dennis Stokes, and Christine Weddle
Consultation: Debbie Entsminger, Karen Yu, Kyu Ho Lee, Melindajoy Mingo, Jolene Blair, Kristie Monteiro, Jon Sween, Bahari Harris, and Leah Wilson-Hartgrove

Some of the anecdotal illustrations in this book are true to life and are included with the permission of the persons involved. All other illustrations are composites of real situations, and any resemblance to people living or dead is coincidental.

Unless otherwise identified, all Scripture quotations in this publication are taken from the HOLY BIBLE: *NEW INTERNATIONAL VERSION®* (NIV®). Copyright © 1973, 1978, 1984 by International Bible Society. Used by permission of Zondervan Publishing House. All rights reserved. Other versions used include: *THE MESSAGE* (MSG). Copyright © 1993, 1994, 1995, 1996, 2000, 2001, 2002, 2005. Used by permission of NavPress Publishing Group; the Holy Bible, *New Living Translation* (NLT), copyright © 1996, 2004. Used by permission of Tyndale House Publishers, Inc., Carol Stream, Illinois 60188. All rights reserved; the *Amplified Bible* (AMP), © The Lockman Foundation 1954, 1958, 1962, 1964, 1965, 1987; The Holy Bible, *New Century Version* (NCV) copyright © 1987, 1988, 1991 by Word Publishing, Dallas, Texas 75039. Used by permission; the *New American Standard Bible* (NASB), © The Lockman Foundation 1960, 1962, 1963, 1968, 1971, 1972, 1973, 1975, 1977, 1995; and *The Living Bible* (TLB), Copyright © 1971, used by permission of Tyndale House Publishers, Inc., Wheaton, IL 60189, all rights reserved.

Printed in China

1 2 3 4 5 6 7 8 / 12 11 10 09 08

Bringing Jesus into My World

RELATIONSHIPS

CONTENTS

INTRODUCTION

In case this is your first study in the Connect series — or even if you've journeyed through other studies before you picked up this one — this overview may help you connect some dots. *GOD: Connecting with His Outrageous Love* is about receiving God's love and loving Him in response. *IDENTITY: Becoming Who God Says I Am* and *SOUL: Embracing My Sexuality and Emotions* are about discovering who God says we are and learning to live out of that true identity. *LIFE: Thriving in a Complex World* is about living well with Jesus. This study is about loving people — all kinds of people. Because if we're loving God and ourselves, then loving people will happen naturally.

CHAPTER FLOW

Think of your time spent in each chapter as a mini-journey . . . an exploratory trip into a significant topic on your way toward authentic spiritual transformation through Jesus. Most chapters in this study have the following sections where you'll "pause" your heart and mind along the way.

A SHORT STORY

Each is based on real life experiences.

PAUSE 1: EXPLORING WHAT GOD SAYS

This section encourages you to look at the Bible to see what God said. We'll include most of the verses for you, from a variety of Bible translations. But nothing beats reading your own Bible to make you comfortable in God's Word. You'll be reading the *New International Version,* unless we say otherwise. Sometime we use *The Message* (MSG), the *New Living Translation* (NLT), the *New Century Version* (NCV), *The Living Bible* (TLB), the *New American Standard Bible* (NASB), or *The Amplified Bible* (AMP). As you move from chapter to chapter, you'll gradually try different approaches to studying, processing, and applying these passages.

PAUSE 2: EXPLORING YOUR REALITY

Our information-driven society makes it easy to walk away from profound truth without considering what it really says about us. This section will guide you as you try to see yourself from God's perspective and explore what it would take for you to become more like Jesus.

PAUSE 3: COMING ALIVE TO GOD AND OTHERS

Our "what's-in-it-for-me?" culture often promotes self-centeredness and shallowness in our relationships. This section will help you examine biblical principles in order to develop patterns of knowing and relating — to Him and to others — with authenticity, honesty, humility, and love.

PAUSE 4: JOURNEYING FORWARD

Being connected with Jesus as your default lifestyle means learning to trust Him with what's true about you — all the way, every day. This section invites you to process and write out what you are learning as you live in Him, as well as what you are doing with what you are learning.

DIGGING DEEPER

Like the photo album you make after a trip, in this optional section you can pause to recap and process the highlights of your experience so far. We'll give you a few "extras" if you want to explore and experience the topic of the chapter more deeply.

IMAGES

In each chapter we've included pictures and artwork to help you reflect on the topics. They are there to stimulate your imagination and heart when words fall short. Take time to gaze at the images and place yourself within these visual stories. If a photo disturbs you, that's okay; try to figure out why.

YOUR JOURNEY THROUGH EACH CHAPTER

For each chapter, expect to devote about an hour to personal preparation — more if you choose to do the optional Digging Deeper section. So pace yourself. You might try working a little at a time on a chapter — say, one section a day or twenty minutes a day — or a longer time of concentrated reflection. After a few chapters you'll find a rhythm that fits you.

FOR GROUP LEADERS

We've provided a leader's guide that can be downloaded at www.NavPress.com. Search for the ISBN or book title.

GETTING YOU STARTED

To get the most from your study, we encourage you to do three simple things:

1. Read the verses meditatively, inviting the Holy Spirit to help you unpack what He wants you to understand from each verse. We've printed most passages from the *New International Version* (NIV), but occasionally quote from other translations for a fresh rendering. You may want to use your own Bible for any or all verses in this study.
2. Mark the verses to help you engage as you read. Be creative! Underline, draw circles or arrows ⟶, highlight, use colored pencils — whatever will help you process as you go.
3. Pray throughout your study, not just when you see a prayer-oriented question. Ask the Lord to shed light on what you're studying and help you connect what you read to the realities in your life.

GUIDELINES FOR SMALL GROUPS

1. Confidentiality: Do not repeat anything said or heard inside the group to anyone outside the group. Refraining from gossip builds trust.
2. Safety: Respect each other's boundaries. Also, accept each other's perceived realities without needing to comment or "fix" how they feel or see things at the moment. Nobody should feel forced to share anything that they prefer to keep private. Providing each other space and supportive care will promote safety.
3. "I" Statements: Be yourself; take off your masks. Share information only about yourself — not "we, they, us, or you."
4. Interference: Avoid giving advice, talking while someone else is sharing, or engaging in subtle competition by saying, "I'm just like you" or by sharing a similar story. Instead, listen attentively, learn from each other's life experiences, and offer brief and affirming feedback.
5. Individuality: Accept and enjoy the diversity in your group, including being at very different places on your spiritual journeys. Allow everyone (but don't force anyone) to discover areas of need or brokenness. Avoid probing or intrusive questioning, as well as tampering with or elaborating on each other's personal sharing.
6. Emotional Sharing: Expect and allow each other to experience a full range of emotion, even if this makes you uncomfortable. This might include crying, raising a voice, or being silent. When this happens, avoid interrupting, communicating that another's feelings are unacceptable or "bad," and touching or hugging without

permission. Allow for times of quiet in your group, because silence can be one of the most powerful healing environments.

7. Roadblocks and Obstacles: It is important to allow people to process their thoughts and feelings without needing to come to clear resolution. It is also normal to experience obstacles and setbacks. Remember that being stuck can be a catalyst for members to move forward. Trust the process!
8. Holy Spirit: Only God can perform the healing and growth needed in our hearts. The purpose of the group is to provide a place where the support, love, and acceptance of God can be modeled and felt, and where the truth of God can be discovered and embraced.
9. Personal Responsibility: Recognize that true life change can only occur with God's help as we yield to His leading. The group can provide accountability through prayer and support.
10. Group Limits: Don't expect your group to provide therapy, counseling, or other in-depth one-to-one support for members. Know when to refer each other to someone outside your group who is better equipped to help.
11. Pace: Some groups study and discuss a complete chapter each week. They prepare all of the questions but only discuss selected ones. Other groups prefer to devote two weeks to each chapter. Find a pace that allows your group to truly meet with God — not just finish an academic exercise.

BENEFITS OF HEALTHY GROUP PROCESS

1. A safe place to share vulnerably and honestly.
2. New relationships.
3. An opportunity to be listened to in an accepting and grace-filled environment.
4. A forum for embracing truth, gaining perspective, and growing spiritually at your own pace.

FOR GROUP DISCUSSION: After reading these guidelines together, discuss this question among you:

Knowing myself, here are several practical things I will do to help make our group a safer place:

-
-
-

In a small group these specific things can make me feel unsafe.

-
-
-

Take time to pray as a group before you begin this journey together.

CHAPTER 1
RECEIVING LOVE TO GIVE LOVE

When Sara looks in the mirror each morning, she avoids her deep brown eyes, as if they were windows into her soul. That way she doesn't have to really see herself. Her own reflection is just too painful. It takes all her energy to hush the criticism she heaps on herself. A glance triggers too many memories, too many shaming thoughts, too much condemnation.

Other people do affirm her now and then . . . for her musical ability, her compassion for kids, her beautiful smile. But Sara doesn't see those things when she looks at herself. She'd rather look at others — her friends in jazz band or the handicapped kids at swim lessons. It's easier to give love to them than to receive love for herself.

Sometimes when she prays, the turmoil inside seems to calm down for a while as she starts to get in touch with God's love for her. Her friends say they like her, and God says He loves her. So why, she agonizes, can't she get it together and allow herself to be loved?

What do you say to yourself about yourself?

Is your self-talk mostly positive or mostly negative? *Explain.*

PAUSE 1_EXPLORING WHAT GOD SAYS

John Eagan writes, "Define yourself radically as one beloved by God. God's love for you and his choice of you constitute your worth. Accept that, and let it become the most important thing in your life" (in *A Traveler Toward the Dawn*, p. 150). The beautiful thing about being God's beloved is that when we're able to receive God's love (and God's love channeled through others), then we can begin loving and accepting ourselves as God loves us. And when our own hearts are full of love from God, then we have enough love to overflow into the hearts of others.

> *1 JOHN 4:10-11,19. This is love: not that we loved God, but that he loved us. . . . Dear friends, since God so loved us, we also ought to love one another. . . . We love because he first loved us.*

How do you think receiving love (from God and others) affects our ability to give love?

Jesus made it clear that His way is based on love.

> *MATTHEW 22:37-40. "Love the Lord your God with all your heart and with all your soul and with all your mind." This is the first and greatest commandment. And the second is like it: "Love your neighbor as yourself." All the Law and the Prophets hang on these two commandments.*

What does this passage imply about loving ourselves?

How does your heart respond to the idea of loving and caring for yourself?

What do you think it feels like . . .

What do you think it looks like . . .

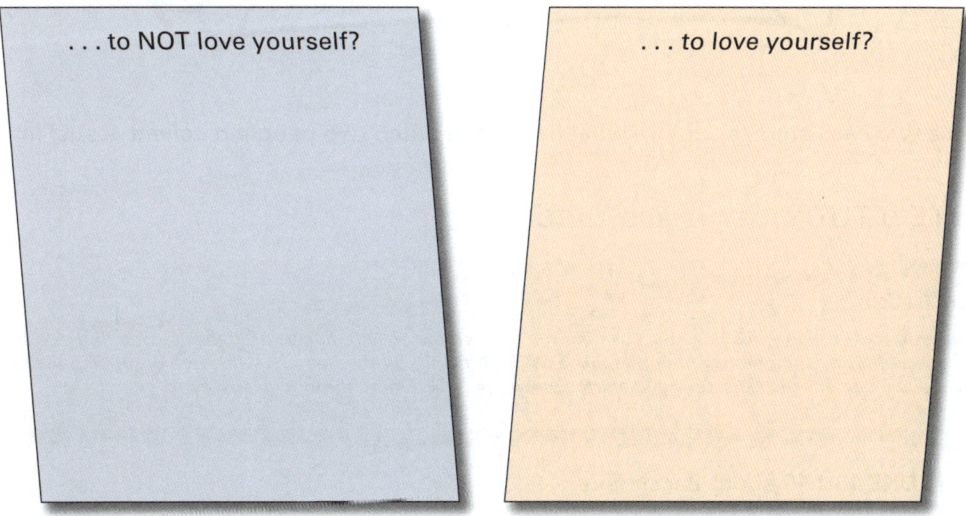

How certain are you that God actually *likes* you (not just loves you because theologically He "has to")?

What barriers may be hindering you from receiving God's love? Write them below.

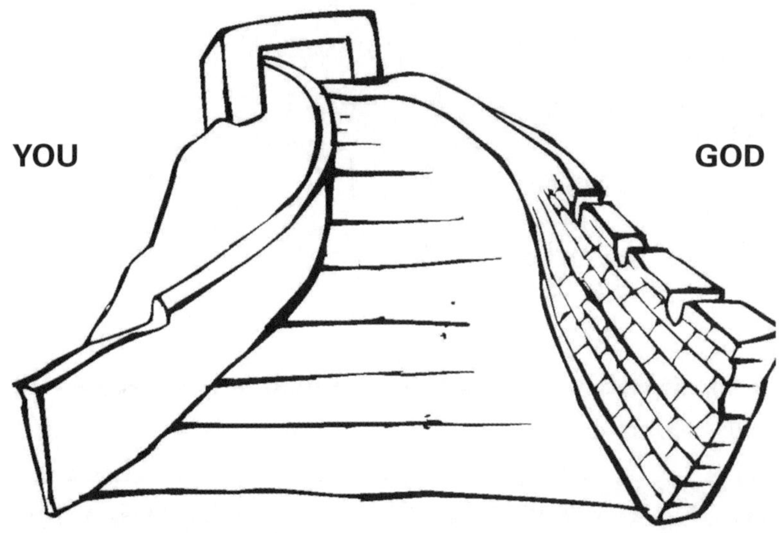

These two case studies explore what happened when two people received Jesus' love.

CASE STUDY: JESUS AND ZACCHAEUS

BACKGROUND

Zacchaeus was probably despised because he was a tax collector. Other Jews probably viewed him as a traitor and a cheat — collecting their money in taxes (plus a cut for himself) for the Romans who were occupying the land. Then Zacchaeus experienced Jesus' love and started viewing himself more through Jesus' eyes.

Read LUKE 19:1-10 about Zacchaeus.

Being the chief tax collector and being hated by his fellow Jews, how do you think Zacchaeus felt about himself?

When Zacchaeus received affirmation and love from Jesus, how do you think it changed the way he felt about himself?

How and why was he able to give of himself for the sake of others?

CASE STUDY: JESUS AND THE GRATEFUL WOMAN

BACKGROUND

The woman who anointed Jesus in this story was unnamed—maybe because of her scandalous past and immoral reputation. Some think she may have been the woman caught in adultery or Mary Magdalene, out of whom Jesus had cast many demons. There's no way to be sure. But somewhere in her journey she had experienced Jesus' love—and she started living out of who Jesus said she was, not who society said she was.

If people know they are loved, they are not afraid of their "badness." They feel accepted and safe, and they do not have to feel "good" about themselves to be safe. Love does that.

—DR. HENRY CLOUD AND DR. JOHN TOWNSEND, *HOW PEOPLE GROW*

Read LUKE 7:36-50 about the woman anointing Jesus' feet.

Being described as an "immoral . . . sinner," how do you think she felt about herself?

When the woman not only heard but received love and affirmation from Jesus, how do you think it changed the way she felt about herself?

How and why was she able to give of herself for the sake of others?

How do you think these exchanges of love between Jesus, Zacchaeus, and the woman may have influenced other people around them?

CONSIDER

Love is a mystery — who can understand it? But God has revealed that loving is at the very heart of the gospel and of life in His kingdom. Here are some fundamentals of love:

- God pours out His jealous love directly into our hearts.
- God also pours His love into our hearts indirectly through the love of others, and through the beauty He created around us.
- If we can receive His love, it helps us love ourselves as He does.
- God uses us to channel His love into others' hearts.

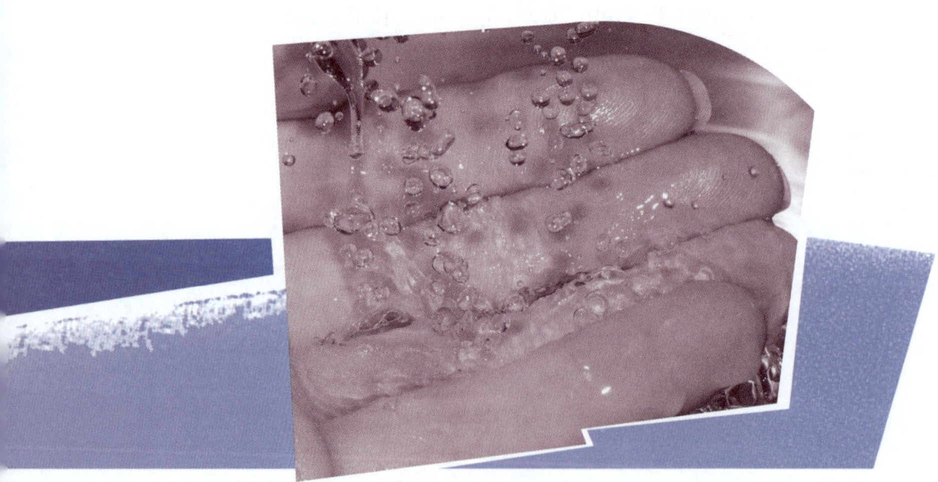

PAUSE 2_EXPLORING YOUR REALITY

Think about it . . . How does a baby know he is loved? Simple: His needs are met! When he's hungry, his mom feeds him. When he's cold, his dad covers him up. When he's frightened, somebody holds him. It was God who created us with needs. Then He gave us the ministry of meeting each other's needs by loving one another. We can't deeply receive love without the humility to accept and admit our needs.

But first we have to admit that we really do have needs. From these verses, how does God feel about our needs?

> *ISAIAH 55:1-3. Come, all you who are thirsty, come to the waters; and you who have no money, come, buy and eat! Come, buy wine and milk without money and without cost. Why spend money on what is not bread, and your labor on what does not satisfy? Listen, listen to me, and eat what is good, and your soul will delight in the richest of fare. Give ear and come to me; hear me, that your soul may live. I will make an everlasting covenant with you, my faithful love promised to David.*

> *PHILIPPIANS 4:19. And my God will meet all your needs according to his glorious riches in Christ Jesus.*

What does God promise to us about meeting our legitimate, God-given human needs?

In the bulleted list below, mark each statement with an "E" (easier for me) or an "H" (harder for me).

When we're ready to receive love, we'll know, because we will begin to experience a process with the following steps:

- I understand that I have needs _____
- I realize that having my needs met is experiencing love _____
- I freely admit that I desire to be loved _____
- I choose to let you love me _____
- I let you love me — on your terms, not mine _____
- I am fulfilled when I have experienced love _____
- I am now able to love others out of my own fulfillment _____

— Thrall, McNicol, and Lynch, *TrueFaced*[1]

[1] Bill Thrall, Bruce McNicol, and John Lynch, *TrueFaced* (Colorado Springs, CO: NavPress, 2004), 85.

Many of us have learned to be so independent that we deny our needs, trying to protect ourselves from disappointment, rejection, abandonment, and so forth. To what extent (if at all) is this true of you?

It's hard for some of us to admit that we really do want and need to be loved — and even harder to ask for it. How do you think men and women might deal with this differently?

For some of us, shame from our culture or our family might prevent us from receiving love or loving ourselves. If this is true of you, explain why.

It's okay to be thirsty and needy — physically and emotionally! List a few personal needs that you've felt recently. How could you invite others and God to show their love to you this week by meeting a genuine need of yours?

> EXAMPLE: I could ask my friends to help me find a new roommate who will be like family to me, and also let them help me pack and move my stuff.

In this quote, Nouwen refers to the "other, louder voices" telling you that you must "earn the love you so desire." When have you felt that way?

> "You are my Beloved, on you my favor rests." That voice has always been there, but it seems that I was much more eager to listen to the other, louder voices saying: "Prove that you are worth something; do something relevant, spectacular or powerful, and then you will earn the love you so desire." Meanwhile, the soft, gentle voice that speaks in the silence and solitude of my heart remained unheard or, at least, unconvincing.
>
> — Henri Nouwen, *Life of the Beloved*[2]

[2] Henri Nouwen, *Life of the Beloved* (New York, NY: The Crossroad Publishing Company, 1992), 28-29.

Do you think of yourself more often as being "beloved" by God and others, or as being a "lover" of God and others, or neither? *Explain.*

Let's get practical. God created you in love and gave you dignity and value. Read each statement about loving and caring for yourself and check your tendencies. If neither, write your own example.

Inner Dialogue	I speak to myself with kind, positive, grace-filled words.	I am critical of myself and speak harsh, condemning words.
Personal Boundaries	I am able to say no to others I respect and care about (even if it might disappoint them) because it is the right thing to do.	I am not able to say no to others, fear disappointing them, and sometimes feel resentful.
Relaxation/ Play	I schedule time to do the things I love to renew my energy.	Because of my responsibilities I find it difficult to relax and don't make time to do the things I love.
Health	I regularly make healthy choices such as nutrition, exercise, or doctor/dental visits.	I am busy working and caring for others and think about myself only when I get sick.
Needing Others	I have a network of friends and family I regularly ask to meet my personal needs.	I am independent and self-reliant and think God alone can meet my needs.
Life Purpose	I have spent time thinking and praying about what I really want to be and do and adjusted my schedule to support that.	I pray that God would get me through the demands of each week and try to live up to others' expectations of me.

Is there an area of your life from the chart above you'd like to change? If so, how can the members in your group support you in doing that?

PAUSE 3_COMING ALIVE TO GOD AND OTHERS

Here's what's so dangerous about not loving ourselves appropriately: We tend to criticize in others what we can't accept in ourselves. Some people would say: "If you spot it, you've got it!"

> *MATTHEW 7:3-5. Why do you look at the speck of sawdust in your brother's eye and pay no attention to the plank in your own eye? How can you say to your brother, "Let me take the speck out of your eye," when all the time there is a plank in your own eye? You hypocrite, first take the plank out of your own eye, and then you will see clearly to remove the speck from your brother's eye.*

CONSIDER: Whenever you get irritated during the next month, look at what you're angry about in someone else, and see if you are doing the same thing, at least in principle.

Think of someone in your everyday life who frequently bugs you. The next time you feel critical of this person, how might you use it as a teachable moment to look inside for your own "specks" or "planks"?

Instead of putting the blame on others, Jesus invites us to bring our weaknesses and flaws out of hiding and into the community of others. That's a big step in loving ourselves. From this list, how is God urging you to recognize the "specks" in your life and begin to expose them to love? Check one or two that seem crucial to you now.

___ Accept a failure or limitation
___ Receive mercy and tenderness
___ Acknowledge a fear or weakness
___ Lovingly own an imperfection in your character
___ Share your anger or sadness with a friend
___ Ask for help or advice
___ Confess a sin
___ Forgive yourself
___ Expose your vulnerability or powerlessness
___ Admit a worry
___ Other?

Love is valuable — so it always comes at a cost. It cost Jesus a lot to love you, right? And it will cost you to "pay it forward" and genuinely love others. It is love's price tag that says to the loved one, "You are infinitely precious and valuable to me!" Read Jesus' call for His followers to willingly pay the cost of following Him and loving others into His kingdom.

Healthy self-denial willingly forbids us from being the central love of our lives because that place is jealously reserved for the Triune God.

> *MATTHEW 10:39. If you cling to your life, you will lose it; but if you give up your life for me, you will find it.* (NLT)
>
> *LUKE 9:23-24. Then he said to them all: "If anyone would come after me, he must deny himself and take up his cross daily and follow me. For whoever wants to save his life will lose it, but whoever loses his life for me will save it."*

How does the world around us urge us to "cling to" or "save" our lives?

How do you feel about denying yourself? Explore any feelings of resistance to this idea.

Of course we can take almost anything to extremes. Sometimes we take "loving ourselves" to the extreme of indulging ourselves with selfishness. Or we take "denying ourselves" to the other extreme of punishing ourselves with self-hatred. Both of these inappropriate ways of loving ourselves come from pride — because life becomes all about us — not about God! Our Father is not in the business of either spoiling or abusing His children.

Which extreme could you tend to lean toward when you get off-balance from healthy self-love? Give an example below of when you've done that.

EXAMPLE: I was just indulging myself when I went into debt to buy more electronics.

SELF-INDULGENCE	**HEALTHY SELF-LOVE**	**SELF-HATRED**

From the verses you just read, and this passage below, what are we promised when we deny ourselves for the sake of others and spend ourselves to meet the needs of others? Circle anything God promises us.

> *ISAIAH 58:9-11. If you do away with the yoke of oppression, with the pointing finger and malicious talk, and if you spend yourselves in behalf of the hungry and satisfy the needs of the oppressed, then your light will rise in the darkness, and your night will become like the noonday. The LORD will guide you always; he will satisfy your needs in a sun-scorched land and will strengthen your frame.*

Imagine if a friend asked you, "Isn't it selfish to love myself when I am called to deny myself, build the kingdom of God, and serve others?" How would you respond to him or her?

> *Healthy self-love is always wrapped in humility. That allows us to see ourselves as God does — as a creature, a sinner, and a new creation in Christ — all at the same time. When we love ourselves appropriately, we don't minimize or magnify our obvious faults. Instead, we embrace the awesome reality that God really does value us highly even in our shameful fallen state. When we believe God's love in our heads and also experience it in our hearts, then we're on the way to loving ourselves.*

PRAYER PAUSE

As you pray, go easy on yourself. It takes a lifetime to fully receive God's love and love your neighbor as yourself. When you doubt who you are, ask the Spirit of God to help you see yourself as "the one Jesus loves." Ask Him to open your heart so you can receive His mercy, love, acceptance, tenderness, and grace. Take time to enjoy and thank God for your belovedness. Ask Him to reveal any resistance, to remove any barriers, and to repair any brokenness in your ability to receive His love and love yourself.

> *Self-rejection is the greatest enemy of the spiritual life because it contradicts the sacred voice that calls us the "Beloved." Being the Beloved expresses the core truth of our existence.*
>
> — HENRI NOUWEN, *LIFE OF THE BELOVED*

PAUSE 4_JOURNEYING FORWARD

It's your life . . . it's your journey. So that means it's up to you how you respond to the ideas in this chapter. Pause 4 in every chapter will be like this one—completely open-ended to invite you to zero in on whatever specifically touched you most. Or whatever disturbed you the most.

Whatever that is, grab on to it—don't gloss over it. During this final Pause, revisit that verse and respond to one or more of the reflective questions. Then pray about what step you should take to "love one another" as Jesus asks us to in the coming week.

At the end of every chapter we'll invite you to select one verse or passage that you read, studied, listened to, or memorized during the week that was meaningful to you. Begin by copying the verse and its reference below, so you'll be able to find it later.

> *1 JOHN 4:10-11. This is love: not that we loved God, but that he loved us. . . . Dear friends, since God so loved us, we also ought to love one another.*

We live in a world of images that deeply influence how we look at life. Choose a picture from this chapter that is meaningful or disturbing to you, and briefly explain why.

How have you experienced God this week?

Then, you'll be invited to select one or more of these reflective questions and journal your response. The point is not to answer all of the questions, but to help focus your reflection on what God is saying to you. Most chapters have a final Journal page to give you space to write.

REFLECTING on what was most meaningful to you from this chapter, respond to one (or more) of these questions in the Journal on the following page:

- What impact does the loving way of Jesus have on your heart?
- As you engage in loving yourself, how might you be setting the stage to love God and others?
- What one action step are you motivated to take in response to what God has taught you?

JOURNAL

Think of the Journal page as part of your spiritual fitness routine. Your spirit, heart, and mind have just finished some vigorous exercise. This is the cool-down phase. Not to be hurried. We suggest two things:

1. Journal on any of the preceding reflective questions.
2. Memorize and meditate on the Scripture memory verse below.

If at all possible, don't leave your study time without capturing in writing the most important things God revealed to you.

SUGGESTED MEMORY VERSE:

RECEIVING LOVE TO GIVE LOVE — MATTHEW 22:39

And the second is like it: "Love your neighbor as yourself."

Last, we'll suggest a key verse on the chapter's topic for you to memorize. If a different verse touched you more, feel free to substitute it. If you take 5–10 minutes right after completing the chapter study to memorize the verse, it will help anchor what you've learned in your heart and mind. After you have memorized the verse, check your accuracy. Try to write the verse from memory in the space below.

DIGGING DEEPER

CASE STUDY: THE FATHER WITH TWO SONS

This familiar story about the father with two sons reveals how people can love themselves inappropriately, and then fail to receive love from others that is there for the taking. As you read the end of the story in LUKE 15:11-32, notice anything that suggests how either son:

. . . RECEIVED (or failed to receive) his father's love.

. . . LOVED (or failed to love) himself or others.

The younger brother may have believed he was loving himself by demanding his "rights." What was the result of his self-focused, prideful love?

When the younger brother concluded that he wasn't "worthy" of being loved, what effect did this have on him? (See verses 19,21.)

Try to get into the older brother's head. What do you imagine he was feeling and saying to himself . . .

. . . ABOUT HIS FATHER? **. . . ABOUT HIS YOUNGER BROTHER?** **. . . ABOUT HIMSELF?**

How did either brother demonstrate self-indulgence or self-hatred?

Imagine being the younger brother the morning after the feast. How do you feel as you consider putting back on the robe, the sandals, and the ring of honor?

Where do you find yourself in this story? Can you relate to the heart of the father, the younger brother, or the older brother? *Explain.*

CHAPTER 2
LOVING OTHERS IN COMMUNITY

Jake felt ashamed of the mess he had gotten himself into. He got caught looking at pornography on the Internet — by the guy he had influenced for Christ. Too embarrassed to talk about it, Jake just backed away quietly — from his friend, from the guys in his Bible study group, from anyone who might bring his secret little habits into the open. Let them think whatever they wanted. It just felt way too risky in his circle of friends to come out of hiding.

Then Jake visited another friend's Bible study group. He was blown away when the leader stood up and said, "Let me introduce the folks who serve with me leading this group. Derreck here overcame a serious drug habit earlier in his life. Susan endured the pain of a messy divorce about five years ago. Jared still struggles with some post-traumatic stress from his stint in Kuwait with the National Guard, but he's gaining altitude. As for me . . . well, I have struggled with depression now and then. And several of us men meet twice a month to help each other stay away from porn. You could say that all of us here are pretty broken people. But we are all experiencing Jesus' healing touch, too. If you'd like to talk with any of us, just give us a call."

Jake was amazed. People actually talked about their "messes" — even the leaders! It had been a long time since he had tasted an authentic environment of grace and truth like this, where people trusted each other and wanted to come closer to Jesus together. Maybe he really didn't have to sort out his mess all by himself. He knew he had some thinking to do about what it really means to love and be transformed within a community of believers.

What (if anything) would attract you to a group of people who relate to each other like these people do?

PAUSE 1_EXPLORING WHAT GOD SAYS

Jesus said that we can't really love God unless we also love people. In fact, one significant proof of our love for God shows up in our relationships with people. His Holy Spirit alive in us draws us and empowers us to love what He loves: humanity . . . every man, woman, and child on earth.

Read the passages below for ways to relate to one another in love — both believers and those among us who are still seeking Him, as well as our families and friends, and even our enemies. Some of these verses address how we feel toward people, while others address how we should (and shouldn't) act.

As you read, underline key phrases that guide how we can relate to others in love. In the columns, write things we should and should not do to offer love to others.

LOVE DOES . . .	PASSAGES	LOVE DOES NOT . . .
Celebrate & grieve with others	ROMANS 12:15-16. Rejoice with those who rejoice; mourn with those who mourn. Live in harmony with one another. Do not be proud, but be willing to associate with people of low position. Do not be conceited. ROMANS 14:19. So let's agree to use all our energy in getting along with each other. Help others with encouraging words; don't drag them down by finding fault. (MSG) ROMANS 15:7. Accept one another, then, just as Christ accepted you, in order to bring praise to God. GALATIANS 6:2. Carry each other's burdens, and in this way you will fulfill the law of Christ. EPHESIANS 4:2. Always be humble and gentle. Be patient with each other, making allowance for each other's faults because of your love. (NLT) EPHESIANS 4:25. Therefore each of you must put off falsehood and speak truthfully to his neighbor, for we are all members of one body. EPHESIANS 4:32. Be kind and compassionate to one another, forgiving each other, just as in Christ God forgave you.	Act superior to others

LOVE DOES . . .	PASSAGES	LOVE DOES NOT . . .
	EPHESIANS 4:15. Instead, speaking the truth in love, we will in all things grow up into him who is the Head, that is, Christ. EPHESIANS 5:21. Submit to one another out of reverence for Christ. 1 THESSALONIANS 5:11. Therefore encourage one another and build each other up, just as in fact you are doing. JAMES 5:16. Therefore confess your sins to each other and pray for each other so that you may be healed. The prayer of a righteous man is powerful and effective. 1 PETER 4:9. Offer hospitality to one another without grumbling.	

Now go back to these verses and check one or two ways of showing love (left column) that come easier to you, and another one or two that are more difficult for you.

From what you wrote above, how would you want somebody else to show you love this week? (Such as praying with you, having a meal with you, encouraging you, listening to your struggles, or helping you with a project.)

Consider this verse:

> *HEBREWS 10:24. And let us consider and give attentive, continuous care to watching over one another, studying how we may stir up (stimulate and incite) to love and helpful deeds and noble activities.* (AMP)

Wherever you hang out with other followers of Christ, how do you see aspects of this passage happening? (Give an example of people caring for each other, stimulating each other to love, or doing helpful deeds.)

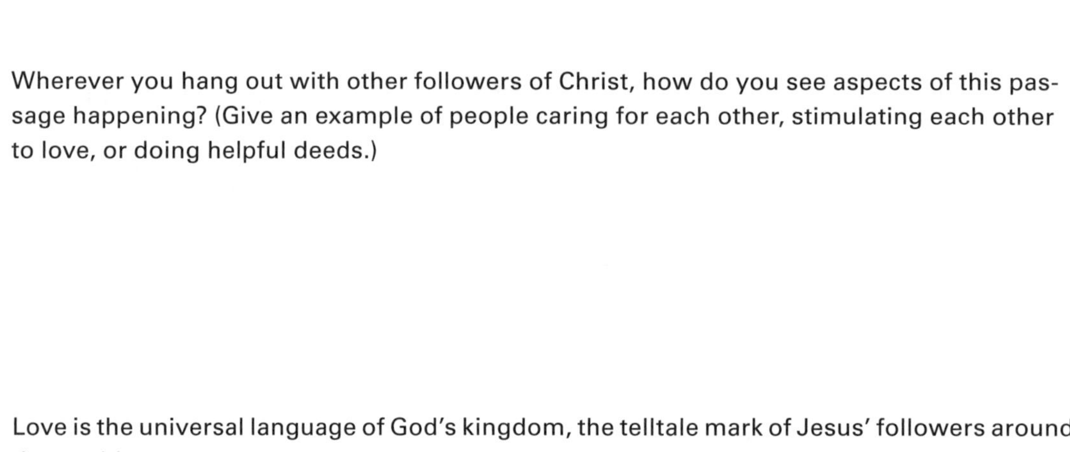

Love is the universal language of God's kingdom, the telltale mark of Jesus' followers around the world.

> *JOHN 13:34-35. A new command I give you: Love one another. As I have loved you, so you must love one another. By this all men will know that you are my disciples, if you love one another.*

Describe a time when you recognized other believers just by their love — not their religious habits or talk.

When we love one another, Jesus' life goes on display through us. How do you think it might impact those among us who haven't met Christ yet if they could see believers loving each other in these ways — and if they could receive love like this?

PAUSE 2_EXPLORING YOUR REALITY

Go back and prayerfully select three verses from Pause 1. Use this chart to help you plan with whom and how you could put them into practice.

VERSE	LOVE WHOM?	BY DOING WHAT?
Example: 1 Thessalonians 5:11 ("encourage & build up")	My younger brother Jason	He's going to run in his first marathon next month, but he's afraid he won't finish. I could call him 2-3 times a week to build up his confidence. And maybe set aside the next two Saturday mornings to run with him. We could memorize 1 Corinthians 9:27 together to quote when he is tempted to quit.

Read GALATIANS 6:9-10. Who should we "do good" to whenever we have an opportunity?

It's natural for almost any community of believers to include some who haven't believed yet but are on a spiritual journey. What communities of believers do you belong to? (Consider your church, Bible study, group of friends, or a ministry team.)

There just is no such thing as a perfect community, a perfect church, a perfect fellowship group, or a perfect family. Does accepting that come easily for you? Or does it make you feel disappointed or disillusioned? *Explain.*

Do you think it is normal or abnormal for people within a typical community of believers to struggle with things like substance addictions, divorce, depression, or pornography, like in the story about Jake? *Explain.*

In your experience, when were you involved in an environment where people didn't exhibit grace and mercy to one another? Describe that experience.

In a community of grace, who I am in God's eyes is not questioned; instead, it is affirmed.

— BILL THRALL, LEADERSHIP CATALYST, INC.

Acceptance often starts "movement" in someone's spiritual growth. In an environment of no condemnation, people are honest about issues they haven't felt safe to reveal before. When they find that it's okay to confess one problem, they fire up the backhoe and they dig deeper into the dark parts of their souls. As acceptance increases, so does confession, and with confession comes intimacy and growth.

— DR. HENRY CLOUD AND DR. JOHN TOWNSEND, *HOW PEOPLE GROW*

When (if ever) have you been in an environment of grace where people trusted each other with their messes (like they do in the Bible study group in the opening story)? How did it affect you and others?

Jesus' way is love, and His love comes to us through the way of the cross — through sacrifice. How do you feel when you sacrifice your comfort, rights, status, money, or time for the good of others?

Where in your life have you been sacrificing for the sake of love? Or in what areas do you need to be more willing to sacrifice in order to love those around you? *Explain.*

Go back and review what you wrote in the chart in Pause 2 — about possible ways to put love into action. Select one of these applications (or any other that God has impressed on you during your study). Write below how you will demonstrate your love for a particular person in the coming week or two.

PAUSE 3_COMING ALIVE TO GOD AND OTHERS

HISTORICAL NOTE

Tertullian was one of the most colorful early Christian scholars. He lived in North Africa about 200 years after Christ died. In AD 197 he wrote a description of life among believers. In it, he told how they used their monthly offerings to support and bury poor people and to supply the needs of destitute orphaned children, elderly people confined in their homes, victims of shipwreck, as well as anyone banished to the islands or shut up in prisons—people who had done nothing wrong except to love God. Observing their lives and "deeds of love," the non-believers around them said, "See how they love one another! See how they are ready even to die for one another!"

—ADAPTED FROM GOSPELCOM.NET

Try to imagine visiting the first generation of Christ's followers as they met in community. These communities were often called *ecclesia* in Greek, often translated as "church." Mark whatever you notice about the ways they showed love for one another.

ACTS 2:44-47. And all the believers lived in a wonderful harmony, holding everything in common. They sold whatever they owned and pooled their resources so that each person's need was met. They followed a daily discipline of worship in the Temple followed by meals at home, every meal a celebration, exuberant and joyful, as they praised God. People in general liked what they saw. Every day their number grew as God added those who were saved. (MSG)

What do you think it was about these people that attracted so many to join them in following Christ?

In his letters to the churches in Rome, Philippi, and Colosse, Paul described lots of ways that they could be showing love to each other. Mark any you notice.

> *ROMANS 12:9-16. Don't just pretend to love others. Really love them. Hate what is wrong. Hold tightly to what is good. Love each other with genuine affection, and take delight in honoring each other. Never be lazy, but work hard and serve the Lord enthusiastically. Rejoice in our confident hope. Be patient in trouble, and keep on praying. When God's people are in need, be ready to help them. Always be eager to practice hospitality. Bless those who persecute you. Don't curse them; pray that God will bless them. Be happy with those who are happy, and weep with those who weep. Live in harmony with each other. Don't be too proud to enjoy the company of ordinary people. And don't think you know it all!* (NLT)

> *PHILIPPIANS 2:1-4. If you have any encouragement from being united with Christ, if any comfort from his love, if any fellowship with the Spirit, if any tenderness and compassion, then make my joy complete by being like-minded, having the same love, being one in spirit and purpose. Do nothing out of selfish ambition or vain conceit, but in humility consider others better than yourselves. Each of you should look not only to your own interests, but also to the interests of others.*

> *COLOSSIANS 3:12-17. Therefore, as God's chosen people, holy and dearly loved, clothe yourselves with compassion, kindness, humility, gentleness and patience. Bear with each other and forgive whatever grievances you may have against one another. Forgive as the Lord forgave you. And over all these virtues put on love, which binds them all together in perfect unity. Let the peace of Christ rule in your hearts, since as members of one body you were called to peace. And be thankful. Let the word of Christ dwell in you richly as you teach and admonish one another with all wisdom, and as you sing psalms, hymns and spiritual songs with gratitude in your hearts to God. And whatever you do, whether in word or deed, do it all in the name of the Lord Jesus, giving thanks to God the Father through him.*

Summarize what loving each other looks like in practice from these passages.

How does "fellowship with the Spirit" (Philippians 2:1) help us to love others this way?

How would you say you're doing in terms of initiating love for people who are different from you in culture, sexual orientation, race, financial status, education, or other ways? What would it look like to "really love them" (Romans 12:9)?

When we live out Jesus' command to love each another, we will influence those outside God's family (if we're not too exclusive!). Why do you think some of us tend to hang out in a "holy huddle" with other followers of Christ?

If we show love for one another — and if we don't — we affect those outside God's family for good or for bad. Consider these two true stories.

In 2004 after the tsunami struck the countries of the Far East, followers of Christ came to minister His love to the devastated survivors through simple acts of service. One of these believers came upon an elderly Muslim man in Sri Lanka who had lost his entire family, his home, and his job. Not knowing what else to do, the believer just sat down next to the elderly man and wept with him. After some time, the man said, "You're a Christian, aren't you?"

"How did you know?" the visitor asked.

"Because you care," the man said through his tears.

(AS TOLD BY MICHAEL CARD)

Mahatma Ghandi is one of the most respected leaders of modern history. A Hindu, Ghandi nevertheless admired Jesus and often quoted from the Sermon on the Mount. Once when the missionary E. Stanley Jones met with Ghandi he asked him, "Mr. Ghandi, though you quote the words of Christ often, why is it that you appear to so adamantly reject becoming his follower?"

Ghandi replied, "Oh, I don't reject your Christ. I love your Christ. It's just that so many of you Christians are so unlike your Christ."

— FROM HTTP://JMM.AAA.NET.AU/ARTICLES/552.HTM

Read GALATIANS 6:8,10. What do these stories illustrate about the power and influence on the world when believers really do offer love to "all people, especially to those who belong to the family of believers" — or when believers fail to love?

PAUSE 4_JOURNEYING FORWARD

1 JOHN 4:10-11. This is love: not that we loved God, but that he loved us. . . . Dear friends, since God so loved us, we also ought to love one another.

Select one verse or passage that was meaningful to you this week and write it here.

We live in a world of images that deeply influence how we look at life. Choose a picture from this chapter that is meaningful or disturbing to you, and briefly explain why.

How have you experienced God this week?

Reflecting on what was most meaningful to you from this chapter, respond to one (or more) of these questions in the Journal on the following page:

- What impact does the loving way of Jesus have on your heart?
- As you and your friends love one another, how might you all be helping others see God and His love?
- What one action step are you motivated to take in response to what God has taught you?

JOURNAL

SUGGESTED MEMORY VERSE:

LOVING ONE ANOTHER —JOHN 13:34-35

A new command I give you: Love one another. As I have loved you, so you must love one another. By this all men will know that you are my disciples, if you love one another.

DIGGING DEEPER (CHOOSE ONE)

1. TOUGH AND TENDER LOVE DRAMA

One believer who had made a mess of his life and needed love from his brothers in Christ was named Onesimus. Read about him in the very short letter (only twenty-five verses) that Paul wrote to PHILEMON, a follower of Jesus who had once owned Onesimus as a slave. Imagine that one of your group members is Philemon, and the rest of you are his friends and leaders in the fellowship that meets in Philemon's house. You are the community of believers who will be receiving Onesimus back in a few days. You've just received Paul's letter. One of you should play the part of Philemon. Two of you think he deserves the legal punishment for a runaway slave — death. The rest of you want to offer mercy and grace along with truth, but you're not sure what that should look like. Have a five-minute impromptu discussion where you consider your options. Also discuss how your decision about Onesimus will help or hinder the sharing of the good news of Jesus in your town and among your families. Then decide how you will receive him back home.

2. TOUGH AND TENDER LOVE DECISION

If it's a stretch for your group to dramatize the return of Onesimus, try considering Jake's situation from the opening story. Imagine that your group was the one he used to attend, and now he has asked to come back and join you again. Take a few minutes to discuss what you should do. What tensions would you need to overcome, and what realities would you likely face in loving Jake with both grace and truth?

3. HOW CAN YOU STRENGTHEN BIBLICAL COMMUNITY?

In your small group, answer these questions together:

1. When was the last time someone spoke a hard truth into your life or the life of another community member? Was it done in love?
2. When was the last time you confessed sin or failures, or shared fears or frustrations, with a safe person in this community?
3. When was the last time you prayed with someone in the community over needs or decisions?
4. When was the last time someone in this community visited you in the hospital, or brought over a meal when you were sick, or met another tangible need?
5. When was the last time a homeless person or someone who was deeply broken was brought into this community and made whole?

Creating and living in community requires people to give up a great deal — time, freedom to do as they like, some privacy, and the desire to protect themselves from being hurt by others. Community is a messy thing, but it is also one of the primary ways God communicates His love to us and to the world.

— ADAPTED FROM ROBERT FINCH, QUOTED BY ALAN ANDREWS AND CHRISTOPHER MORTON

CHAPTER 3
RESTORING BROKEN RELATIONSHIPS

For years Carlos smothered under a ton of hurt that his older brothers had heaped on him. Long ago he decided to protect his heart by refusing to forgive them. Carlos went silent with his pain and avoided the stirrings in his heart regarding his unforgiveness, growing resentment, and simmering anger. Shutting his brothers out of his life was his way of getting even. Now, as a grown man, frankly, it just exhausted him.

Then he was confronted with the words of Jesus in Matthew 6:14-16: "For if you forgive men for their transgressions, your heavenly Father will also forgive you. But if you do not forgive men, then your Father will not forgive your transgressions." That really raised the stakes for Carlos. Disobeying his heavenly Father by withholding forgiveness from his brothers . . . well, that seemed like a lose-lose scenario. But if he broke his silence and tried to reconnect, wasn't he just setting himself up for more rejection?

While he struggled with this, Carlos felt something inside him begin to break. He just didn't want his resentment to control him anymore. How could he begin to forgive them, yet set boundaries with his brothers? Maybe this personal breaking was the strange first step toward restoration. The risk of further pain from his brothers seemed like a small thing compared to rejecting forgiveness from his heavenly Father.

If you were in Carlos's situation, what would you do?

PAUSE 1_EXPLORING WHAT GOD SAYS

Loving one another is a wonderful ideal — until something goes wrong. Paul advised the believers in Rome to blend hope with realism when he wrote: "If it is possible, as far as it depends on you, live at peace with everyone" (Romans 12:18). Frankly, peace and restored trust aren't always possible. But this chapter will help you explore your part in healing broken relationships.

Is there someone whose relationship with you is strained or broken today? If so, place his/her first initial here: ________________

Mark on the continuum below how you rate the seriousness of the problem between the two of you.

←——————————————————————————————→

DEEP WOUNDING **SERIOUS CONFLICT** **MINOR IRRITATION**

This chapter will highlight ways of handling conflicts and a process of restoring relationships. (The CONNECT study *SOUL: Embracing My Sexuality and Emotions* addresses trusting God for healing of deep wounding.) As you work through this chapter, ask God to show you your next step in healing this broken relationship.

God's Word says a lot about the causes of broken relationships. As you meditate on this passage, highlight or circle anything you notice that may be contributing to the conflict you just mentioned.

> *EPHESIANS 4:25-32. Therefore each of you must put off falsehood and speak truthfully to his neighbor, for we are all members of one body. "In your anger do not sin." Do not let the sun go down while you are still angry, and do not give the devil a foothold. He who has been stealing must steal no longer, but must work, doing something useful with his own hands, that he may have something to share with those in need. Do not let any unwholesome talk come out of your mouths, but only what is helpful for building others up according to their needs, that it may benefit those who listen. And do not grieve the Holy Spirit of God, with whom you were sealed for the day of redemption. Get rid of all bitterness, rage and anger, brawling and slander, along with every form of malice. Be kind and compassionate to one another, forgiving each other, just as in Christ God forgave you.*

Has this passage identified something you've done to add fuel to the conflict? If so, explain.

EXAMPLE: I was really bad-mouthing Matt to my girlfriend last night ("unwholesome talk"—verse 29). He didn't hear it, but it just reinforced my own bad attitude.

YOUR EXAMPLE:

Has this passage identified something you could do to begin bridging the gap between you?

EXAMPLE: I can stop saying to others things I'm not sure are true about him.

YOUR EXAMPLE:

Why do you think working through bitterness (verse 31) comes before forgiving each other (verse 32)?

In healing relationships among followers of Jesus, what difference does it make knowing that . . .

. . . "we are all members of one body" (verse 25)?

. . . "in Christ God forgave you" (verse 32)?

WHO MAKES THE FIRST MOVE?

According to these verses, resolving conflict involves admitting that we've offended someone — or someone has offended us.

> *MATTHEW 5:23. If you enter your place of worship and, about to make an offering, you suddenly remember a grudge a friend has against you, abandon your offering, leave immediately, go to this friend and make things right. Then and only then, come back and work things out with God.* (MSG)
>
> *MATTHEW 18:15-16. If your brother sins against you, go and show him his fault, just between the two of you. If he listens to you, you have won your brother over. But if he will not listen, take one or two others along, so that "every matter may be established by the testimony of two or three witnesses."*

According to these verses, who needs to make the first move in a conflict — the offender or the one who was offended? Why?

Who needs to know about your conflict, and in what order?

RESTORATION IS A PROCESS

Forgiveness is simply choosing to do the right thing. It heals instead of hurts, restores broken relationships, and substitutes love where there was hate.

— GERALD SITTSER, *A GRACE DISGUISED*

Restoring broken relationships involves authentically facing anger, hurts, and bitterness, and then moving to forgiveness, repentance, reconciliation, trust, and restoration. Match the terms on the left with their definitions on the right. (All definitions are from *American Heritage Dictionary*. Answers are at the end of Pause 1.)

____ *Forgiving*	A. Re-establishing friendship; choosing to relate again
____ *Repenting*	B. Having confidence in someone's integrity, ability, character, and truthfulness
____ *Reconciling*	C. Excusing someone for a fault or offense; renouncing your anger or resentment; absolving someone from payment
____ *Trusting*	D. Having genuine sorrow for your past conduct or sin, and turning away from it
____ *Restoring*	E. Bringing back to the original condition

Forgiveness doesn't depend on others; it can be just between you and God if the other person is unwilling. When others show repentance, reconciliation can begin. Then if they earn trust, restoration can begin. Sometimes trust will never be restored.

Is there someone you need to forgive who doesn't see a reason (or is unwilling) to ask for forgiveness? *Explain.*

Reconciliation involves two. Do not think that because you have forgiven that you have to reconcile. You can offer reconciliation, but it must be contingent upon the other person owning her behavior and bringing forth trustworthy fruits.

— DR. HENRY CLOUD AND DR. JOHN TOWNSEND, *BOUNDARIES*

What might be in it for you to forgive someone who isn't sorry or who hasn't asked for forgiveness yet?

CASE STUDY: JOSEPH AND HIS BROTHERS

BACKGROUND

About 3,700 years ago, Joseph (like Carlos in the opening story) struggled with forgiving his brothers for years of rejection and injustice. They even sold him into slavery and he ended up in prison. That's where he was when the Egyptian authorities spotted him and eventually raised him to a place of power and influence in Egypt — second only to the Pharaoh! When a terrible famine struck, God used Joseph's gifts to save the lives of millions of Egyptians, as well as his entire Jewish family. Joseph could easily have used his power to get even with his cruel brothers. But he refused to allow injustice to turn him into a bitter person. Instead, he worked through his issues and — in his mature years — forgave his brothers. (If you want to read more of the story of Joseph, see Genesis chapters 37; 39–50.)

Read GENESIS 50:15-21. Why do you think Joseph cried so much (mentioned at least seven times in the full story)?

In the process of forgiveness, the people involved aren't always at the same point at the same time. One may be ready to be restored while the other is still struggling to trust. At this point in the story above (Genesis 50), where do you think Joseph was in the process of forgiveness?

Where do you see his brothers in the process?

What perspective helped Joseph overcome the pains of injustice at the hands of his brothers (verse 20)?

Over time, have you ever experienced God's goodness come out of an experience of suffering or conflict? *Explain.*

God calls His children to a countercultural lifestyle of forgiveness in a world that demands an eye for an eye — and worse. But if loving God is the first commandment, and loving our neighbor proves our love for God, and if it is easy to love those who love us, then loving our enemies must be the filial badge that identifies Abba's children. Only reckless confidence in a Source greater than ourselves can empower us to forgive the wounds inflicted by others.

— BRENNAN MANNING, *THE RABBI'S HEARTBEAT*

[Answers for page 47: C-Forgiving, D-Repenting, A-Reconciling, B-Trusting, E-Restoring.]

PAUSE 2_EXPLORING YOUR REALITY

WHAT WOULD YOU DO?

Select one of the following scenarios. Decide as a group what suggestions you'd offer, such as forgiveness only, forgiveness and reconciliation, or how trust could be earned again on the way to restoration.

1. Felicia and Chantel have had lots of conflicts in the past. But this time it got really ugly. Felicia said she would help Chantel move, but then she changed her mind at the last minute. Chantel told her in pretty graphic terms to "go to hell," and is still bad-mouthing Felicia to all their friends a month later. What would you recommend to each of them?	2. Jason and Mike are friends and have always enjoyed working together in the past. That is, until Jason took credit for Mike's profits and beat Mike out of the promotion they both wanted. Tension is growing, and Mike feels betrayed, so he's avoiding Jason at work. He just got an e-mail from Jason saying, "Can we talk?" What would you recommend to each of them?
Your Group's Advice to Each Person:	Your Group's Advice to Each Person:

PERSONAL APPLICATION

NOW think about the person you identified in Pause 1 with whom you are experiencing a broken relationship. What has God been saying to you so far about this conflict?

No matter who you think was most at fault, what can you do to begin the healing process — to ask for and offer forgiveness, and move toward reconciliation and restoration (if appropriate)?

Forgiving others ultimately brings freedom, but it also costs. That's because forgiveness involves facing some real stuff. It is the process of giving up what we feel somebody owes us, grieving over what we did not get, and coming alive to how we were hurt. What do you think is the biggest thing it might cost you to seek forgiveness and move toward mending your relationship?

On the other hand, what do you think it would cost you not to forgive?

Who from your small group or community of faith can support you as you move toward forgiveness and reconciliation? ____________________ How do you want this person to support you? Check your top three.

____ listen to you without judgment as you express your anger or hurt
____ help you process your feelings about the broken relationship
____ affirm any steps of progress you make
____ sit with you as you contact the other person
____ pray with and for you when you meet with the other person
____ help you determine if and when reconciliation and restoration are appropriate
____ help you keep on forgiving if the hurt or anger resurfaces
____ refrain from gossip about you, and refrain from bad-mouthing the other person
____ other support?

How do you think those outside God's family may be influenced if you choose to forgive and mend this relationship — or if you choose not to?

What freedom and healing do you think are awaiting you as you begin to mend this relationship?

PRAYER PAUSE

Spend some time praying over a specific strained relationship(s) in your life. Take the following questions to God, and ask Him to open your eyes to the truth about your relationships.

- ☐ Lord, is there anyone I need to go to and ask for forgiveness so that our relationship can be restored?
- ☐ Lord, is there anyone I need to go to and offer forgiveness?
- ☐ Lord, is there anything I need to forgive myself for?
- ☐ Lord, what barriers or fears (if any) are keeping me from asking for, offering, or receiving forgiveness?
- ☐ Lord, who (besides You) should I get support from as I take steps to forgive and reconcile?

Ask God to guide you in the next step on your journey of forgiveness of sin and reconciliation of relationships.

PAUSE 3_COMING ALIVE TO GOD AND OTHERS

It is the tension between God's justice and mercy that makes God so capable of dealing with wrongdoers. God is able to punish people without destroying them, and to forgive people without indulging them. . . . Mercy does not abrogate justice; it transcends it.

— GERALD SITTSER, *A GRACE DISGUISED*

OTHERS

We humans can be strangely inconsistent. When I hurt you, I want to receive mercy. But when you hurt me, I want you to get justice for it — not mercy! Jesus came to bring both, restoring us to the Father. In Jesus' kingdom, mercy overcomes judgment and thus satisfies the demand for justice — just as it did at the cross.

MERCY	JUSTICE	GRACE
Withholding punishment you deserve	Getting what you deserve	Receiving kindness that you don't deserve

Read the story of forgiveness from MATTHEW 18:21-35.

In this parable, did you notice that the first servant deserved justice (verse 25)? But he begged for mercy (verse 26), and was given both mercy and grace (verse 27) — not justice.

When his fellow servant begged him for mercy (verse 29), why do you think he couldn't or wouldn't show mercy?

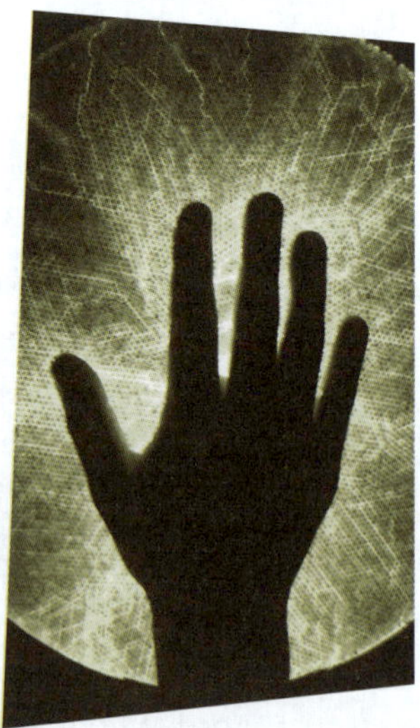

What does "seventy times seven" suggest to you about the nature of forgiveness (verse 22)?

In chapter 1 you explored the principle that we love because He first loved us (1 John 4:19). What similar principle does Jesus' parable here reveal about mercy (verse 33)?

Though forgiveness appears to contradict what seems fair and right, forgiving people decide that they would rather live in a merciful universe than in a fair one, for their sake as much as for anyone else's.

— GERALD SITTSER, *A GRACE DISGUISED*

Which would you rather live in: a world that's merciful, or a world that's fair? *Explain.*

When we are in conflict, it is natural to want justice and to feel angry. Ecclesiastes 3:8 says, "There is a time to love and a time to hate." Sometimes as we awaken from emotional numbness into the forgiveness process, we need a season to hate the wrong done to us. But we can't stay there forever. If we get stuck in our demand for justice, we are in danger of becoming bitter.

> *JAMES 2:12-13. So whatever you say or whatever you do, remember that you will be judged by the law that sets you free. There will be no mercy for those who have not shown mercy to others. But if you have been merciful, God will be merciful when he judges you.* (NLT)

Why does mercy win out over judgment?

Huge on God's agenda for us is to "overcome evil with good" (Romans 12:21) — especially with our enemies. Mark ways we can do that.

> *ROMANS 12:17-20. Never pay back evil with more evil. Do things in such a way that everyone can see you are honorable. Do all that you can to live in peace with everyone. Dear friends, never take revenge. Leave that to the righteous anger of God. For the Scriptures say, "I will take revenge; I will pay them back," says the LORD. Instead,*

"If your enemies are hungry, feed them. If they are thirsty, give them something to drink. In doing this, you will heap burning coals of shame on their heads." (NLT)

Is there anyone in your daily life who might be your personal "enemy" (i.e. attitude of hostility)?

A cultural or historical enemy feels hostility toward you because you represent a group he finds offensive, not necessarily because of anything you have done to him personally.

Who might consider you (or people like you) as a cultural/historical enemy?

What historical/cultural enemies might you have?

What might it look like in practical ways for you to "do good" to an enemy of yours?

PRAYER PAUSE

As you pray, ask God to reveal any anger, bitterness, fear, or numbness in your heart toward someone who has hurt you. Stay in prayer awhile. Ask Him to show you the next step in your journey of forgiveness, healing, and restoration of relationships.

When forgiveness seems impossible, we can remember this: Jesus Christ lives in us, and he can do what we cannot. As so we cling to the promise, "With God all things are possible."

— STEPHEN ARTERBURN AND DAVID STOOP, *SEVEN KEYS TO SPIRITUAL RENEWAL*

PAUSE 4_JOURNEYING FORWARD

1 JOHN 4:10-11. This is love: not that we loved God, but that he loved us. . . . Dear friends, since God so loved us, we also ought to love one another.

Select one verse or passage that was meaningful to you this week and write it here.

We live in a world of images that deeply influence how we look at life. Choose a picture from this chapter that is meaningful or disturbing to you, and briefly explain why.

How have you experienced God this week?

Reflecting on what was most meaningful to you from this chapter, respond to one (or more) of these questions in the Journal on the following page:

- What impact does the loving way of Jesus have on your heart?
- As you and your friends love one another, how might you all be helping others see God and His love?
- What one action step are you motivated to take in response to what God has taught you?

JOURNAL

SUGGESTED MEMORY VERSE:

FORGIVING EACH OTHER — EPHESIANS 4:32, NLT

Instead, be kind to each other, tenderhearted, forgiving one another, just as God through Christ has forgiven you.

DIGGING DEEPER: PATHWAYS TO RESTORATION

Most of our conflicts aren't as devastating as Joseph's (Pause 1), but they still hurt. Here are some communication pathways to try when you're resolving an ordinary, everyday conflict before it seriously damages the relationship.

PATHWAY ONE: Recognize and put words to your hurts. Sometimes we stuff our anger when we've been hurt; at other times, we just go numb. But buried hurts are buried alive! So put words to your hurt: "I feel abandoned by her because she . . ." or "I feel betrayed because he . . ."

PATHWAY TWO: Talk to God about your hurts. Sometimes we forget that God listens to the cries of our hearts and understands our pain. His presence can comfort us if we will go to Him honestly with our hurts. The Holy Spirit is our Comforter (John 15:26). Ask the Holy Spirit to comfort your heart in regard to these specific hurts.

PATHWAY THREE: Seek outside counsel or mediation. At any point in the process of relational restoration, consider asking for help. Deeper conflicts and more serious hurts may need the help of trusted others to come alongside. Gifted people within the body of Christ can help during these conflicts.

PATHWAY FOUR: Embrace the ways of Jesus in broken relationships. Jesus came to heal the broken relationship between God and humanity. He came in amazing humility and offered us mercy and forgiveness — again and again and again. Embracing the way of Jesus means humbling ourselves enough to offer mercy and forgiveness to those who hurt us, whether they ask for it or not.

PATHWAY FIVE: Take the initiative to talk to the person face-to-face. Avoid the gossip trail along with complaining to others. Take the initiative by making the first move to open up a conversation about your issue, regardless of whose "fault" it seems to be. If possible, talk face-to-face.

PATHWAY SIX: Declare the importance of the relationship. The relationship should be more important to you than getting your way or getting justice or proving who's right. Tell the other person that "Our relationship is very important to me, and I don't want this temporary problem to get between us."

PATHWAY SEVEN: Seek to resolve hurts before solving the problem. Before you try to resolve the problem or issue that caused the conflict, discuss the pain you feel. For instance, instead of saying, "I think you were wrong to take money from me without asking," you could say, "When you took money from me without asking, I felt like you violated my space. I felt betrayed." That lets you begin the discussion about relational trust before you get to personal property rights. Expect both of you to have hurts because one's reaction to the problem may have hurt the other. After admitting hurts, apologize and ask for forgiveness. Accept one another's apologies, and speak words of forgiveness.

PATHWAY EIGHT: Talk about the problem and seek a generic solution. Now you're ready to discuss the initial problem. One way is to ask, "How will we handle this in the future?" Keep the conversation open until you come up with an approach that works for both of you.

PATHWAY NINE: Pray and do something together. If possible, pray together. Thank God for each other. Ask God to forgive you. Do something together soon that you would normally do (like go out for pizza) to rebuild a sense of openness and trust between you.

CHAPTER 4
LOVING WITHIN FAMILIES

Families today are very diverse and may look very different: traditional, blended, biracial, foster, gay, group home, hotel, etc. Read the following statistics about families in the United States since 2000. Check one statistic that surprises you.

A GLIMPSE AT AMERICAN HOUSEHOLDS[1]

Single Parents

- One in two children will live in a single-parent family at some point in childhood.
- One in three children is born to unmarried parents.

Divorced Parents

- Each year more than one million children have parents who separate or divorce.
- More than half of Americans today have been, are, or will be in one or more step-family situations.

Guardians/Foster Care

- One child out of 25 lives with neither parent.
- An estimated 550,000 children are in foster care.
- 2.4 million grandparents are the primary caregivers for the children in their families.

---

[1] Statistics are compiled from U.S. Census Bureau of Household and Family Statistics, 2000; *New York Times*, May 20, 2001, Jane Fritsch; State of America's Children Yearbook 2000, Children's Defense Fund; National Survey of America's Families; The National Commission on Children; Stepfamily Association of America; CRS Report for Congress: Foster Care and Adoption Statistics; U.S. Census Bureau Press Release; National Adoption Information Clearinghouse; U.S. State Department; American Bar Association, 1987, Children of Lesbians and Gays Everywhere (COLAGE); Council on Contemporary Families.

Adoption

- One million children in the United States live with adoptive parents.
- More than 100,000 children are adopted each year.

Gay and Lesbian–Headed Households

- One-third of lesbian households and one-fifth of gay male households have children.

Over your lifespan, you'll probably be a part of several different families (such as your childhood family, a foster or group home, your spouse and in-laws, etc.). You may have come from a close-knit, nurturing, healthy family. On the other hand, you may not even consider the people you are living with as "family." Since we live on a fallen planet, every family has dysfunctions, which can leave us with feelings of disappointment (or worse) over how we were raised. But God can use the family you are in for good, no matter how flawed it may be. Living in and loving well within our families is a significant part of our lifelong journey and process of spiritual transformation.

What do you think are some of the purposes and benefits of being in a family?

PAUSE 1_EXPLORING WHAT GOD SAYS

In this chapter you will look at the relationships between parents and children, and between husbands and wives. These foundational relationships affect every other relationship in life.

From these passages, mark whatever you notice about healthy parent-child relationships.

> *EPHESIANS 6:1-4. Children, obey your parents in the Lord [as His representatives], for this is just and right. Honor (esteem and value as precious) your father and your mother—this is the first commandment with a promise—that all may be well with you and that you may live long on the earth. Fathers, do not irritate and provoke your children to anger [do not exasperate them to resentment], but rear them [tenderly] in the training and discipline and the counsel and admonition of the Lord.* (AMP)
>
> *1 TIMOTHY 5:3-4. Give proper recognition to [take care of—*MSG*] those widows who are really in need. But if a widow has children or grandchildren, these should learn first of all to put their religion into practice by caring for their own family and so repaying their parents and grandparents, for this is pleasing to God.*

Summarize what you observed about healthy parent-child relationships. What do these passages have to say to children (of any age)?

What do they have to say to parents?

God commands us to honor our parents regardless of their performance, behavior, or dysfunction. Why? Because honoring parents demands that we live by faith — we have to trust God in His sovereign wisdom will use our parents to help shape us into the people He wants us to be. . . . Honoring your parents does not mean endorsing irresponsibility or sin. It is not a denial of what your parents have done wrong. Honoring your parents is an attitude accompanied by actions that says to your parents: "You are worthy. You have value. You are the person God sovereignly placed in my life. You may have failed me, hurt me, and disappointed me at times, but I am taking off my judicial robe and releasing you from the courtroom of my mind. I choose to look at you with compassion — as people with needs, concerns, and scars of your own."

— DENNIS RAINEY, *THE TRIBUTE*

Think about the ideas in the Rainey quote. Where are you on your journey of trusting God with whatever parents you have?

Why do you think God asks you to "honor" your parents throughout life? (Notice His promise in Ephesians 6:2.)

How is "honor" different from "obedience"?

CASE STUDY: THE FAMILIES OF DAVID

Maybe you've studied about David before — the glorious king of Israel, leader of mighty men, writer of psalms, and a "man after God's own heart." The Bible shows that he finished his life as an influential man deeply connected with God. But have you ever taken a look at his various families — the one he grew up in, the stepfamily he was "adopted" into, or the one he raised with his different wives? It makes your heart break, and proves that dysfunctional families have been around for thousands of years! As you read the story of David and his imperfect family life, meditate on how God still chose to work out His plan in the midst of this extended family's brokenness.

SCENE 1: The family David was raised in

READ 1 SAMUEL 16:1-13 and 1 SAMUEL 17:28-31.

David was anointed by Samuel to be the future king of Israel (verse 13). How do you think that might have affected his relationship with his family?

What rejection and abandonment do you think David may have experienced in his younger years from his father and older brothers?

How (if at all) can you identify emotionally with this part of David's family life?

SCENE 2: The family David was "adopted" into

READ 1 SAMUEL 16:14-23 and 1 SAMUEL 18:1-12,27-29.

King Saul invited David as a young man to live in his house, first as a musician, then as his personal armor-bearer, and eventually as his son-in-law. How did David experience additional rejection and abuse from Saul?

How was Jonathan a better brother to David than his own natural brothers?

How (if at all) can you identify emotionally with this part of David's family life?

PAUSE 2_EXPLORING YOUR REALITY

Today I wonder why it is God refers to Himself as "Father" at all. This, to me, in light of the earthly representation of the role, seems a marketing mistake. Why would God want to call Himself Father when so many fathers abandon their children? As a child, the title Father God offered an ambiguous haze with which to interact. I understood what a father did as well as I understood the task of a shepherd. All the vocabulary about God seemed to come from ancient history, before video games, palm pilots, and the internet.

— DONALD MILLER, *BLUE LIKE JAZZ*

LOOKING BACK ON YOUR FAMILY

How can you relate to the quote above (if at all)?

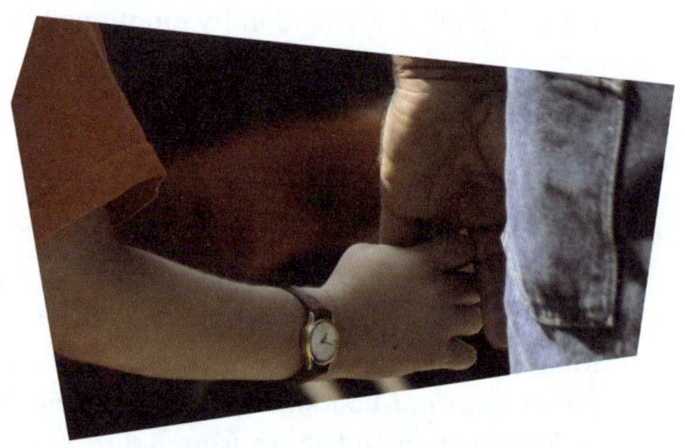

Draw or briefly describe the family of your childhood.

How might your past relationships with your parents or caregivers be affecting your current relationship with God?

Looking back, what other influences besides your parents (such as other people, movies, books, TV shows, music, or other events) have shaped your current view of family and marriage? Explain how they influenced you.

LOOKING AT YOUR FAMILY NOW

Think about how you were parented. What impact is that having now on how you relate to children, your spouse (or boyfriend or girlfriend), or friends?

Describe your current relationship with your parents (or those in a parenting role).

HONORING YOUR PARENTS MEANS:

- Choosing to place great value on your relationship with them.
- Taking the initiative to improve your relationship.
- Obeying them until you establish yourself as an adult.
- Recognizing what they've done right in your life.
- Recognizing the sacrifices they have made for you.
- Praising them for the legacy they are passing on to you.
- Seeing them through the eyes of Christ, with understanding and compassion.
- Forgiving them as Christ has forgiven you.

— DENNIS RAINEY, *THE TRIBUTE*[2]

[2] Dennis Rainey with David Boehi, *The Tribute: What Every Parent Wants to Hear* (Nashville, TN: Thomas Nelson, 1994), 39.

From this list or your own ideas, what is one practical way you want to show honor to your parents, even if they've done things that have hurt you or others?

What is one change you want or need to make in your relationships with family members? Include your first practical step.

LOOKING AHEAD TO YOUR FUTURE FAMILY

As you look toward your future family, check any ideas below that describe how you feel:

____ Families don't work.

____ In this world of war, terrorism, and disease, why would I want my child to go through so much pain?

____ I really don't have a clue how to be a good parent, so I don't plan to have kids.

____ I'm trusting God for a godly spouse and maybe children, too, if He gives them.

____ If a family happens, it happens. I'll cross that bridge when I come to it.

____ Other feelings?

When you imagine yourself as a spouse or a parent, is there anything you are anxious or fearful about? If so, express it here.

We can't change or control our beginnings. But we can work with God to create a positive future. You could be the start of a new spiritual generation in your family! What is one way you can prepare now for a healthier, more satisfying family life in the future?

Has God given you friends or older mentors to be "family" to you? If so, who?

How can you be a temporary "family" for someone who needs you?

PSALM 68:5-6. A father to the fatherless, a defender of widows, is God in his holy dwelling. God sets the lonely in families.

PRAYER PAUSE

Spend time talking with God about the family and relatives He has given you. Listen to what He is saying to you about your relationship with your family; be aware of what your heart is experiencing. Ask God to draw them deeply into His love for them.

Also pray for your kids (present and future, spiritual and physical), future spouses for your kids, and your grandkids, even if they don't exist yet. Talk with God about your hope and desire to raise families and generations who will honor Him and have a heart to serve Him.

As you begin to see and understand the missing element in the [parenting] you received, your responsibility is to grieve and forgive so that you may be healed of whatever your [parents] might have done wrong. Then, as you see and take responsibility for your side of the problem, you will be able to receive what you did not get, gain control, and change those areas where life has not worked for you thus far. In this twofold process of forgiveness and responsibility, you will find unlimited growth.

— DR. HENRY CLOUD AND DR. JOHN TOWNSEND, *THE MOM FACTOR*

Pray about what kind of parent you are now — or would like to become some day. If you had a broken or absent family, take time to grieve and forgive. Also ask God to put others in your life to meet the needs your family was unable to meet.

PAUSE 3_COMING ALIVE TO GOD AND OTHERS

In addition to the parent-child relationship, the husband-wife relationship[3] is at the core of family life. So where does marriage fit in your personal journey? Have you already found your life partner, or are you still looking? Some of us live in a fantasy world, convinced that our dream partner will banish our loneliness forever. Others have given up on marriage or have settled for the practical benefits (sex or financial security) rather than hoping for love and deep friendship in marriage. Wherever you are now, the Bible portrays a fulfilling marriage (along with contented singleness) as real possibilities in God's family.

MARRIAGE

How would you describe the relationship between your parents (or other marriages you've observed)? How has this influenced the way you view marriage today?

In these verses, circle or highlight any words that describe what God wants husbands to be and do for their wives.

EPHESIANS 5:21,25-33. Be subject to one another out of reverence for Christ (the Messiah, the Anointed One). (AMP) . . .

Husbands, love your wives, just as Christ loved the church and gave himself up for her to make her holy, cleansing her by the washing with water through the word, and to present her to himself as a radiant church, without stain or wrinkle or any other blemish, but holy and blameless. In this same way, husbands ought to love their wives as their own bodies. He who loves his wife loves himself. After all, no one ever hated his own body, but he feeds and cares for it, just as Christ does the church — for we are members of his body. "For this reason a man will leave his father and mother and be united to his wife, and the two will become one flesh." This is a profound mystery — but I am talking about Christ and the church. (NIV) *However, let each man of you [without exception] love his wife as [being in a sense] his very own self.* (AMP)

1 PETER 3:7. In the same way, you husbands must give honor to your wives. Treat your wife with understanding as you live together. She may be weaker than you are, but she is your equal partner in God's gift of new life. Treat her as you should so your prayers will not be hindered. (NLT)

---

[3] In other CONNECT studies you can explore in more depth the broader themes of man-woman relationships and singleness.

Now study these verses written to wives. Circle or highlight any words that describe what God wants wives to be and do for their husbands.

> *EPHESIANS 5:21-24,33. [for wives] Be subject to one another out of reverence for Christ (the Messiah, the Anointed One).* (AMP) *Wives, submit to your husbands as to the Lord. For the husband is the head of the wife as Christ is the head of the church, his body, of which he is the Savior. Now as the church submits to Christ, so also wives should submit to their husbands in everything.* (NIV) *. . . Let the wife see that she respects and reverences her husband [that she notices him, regards him, honors him, prefers him, venerates and esteems him; and that she defers to him, praises him, and loves and admires him exceedingly].* (AMP)

> *1 PETER 3:1-4. In the same way, you wives must accept the authority of your husbands. Then, even if some refuse to obey the Good News, your godly lives will speak to them without any words. They will be won over by observing your pure and reverent lives. Don't be concerned about the outward beauty of fancy hairstyles, expensive jewelry, or beautiful clothes. You should clothe yourselves instead with the beauty that comes from within, the unfading beauty of a gentle and quiet spirit [unanxious or unintimidated —* MSG*], which is so precious to God.* (NLT)

From these passages, what part do unselfishness and sacrificial love play in marriage?

What lingering questions, concerns, or unresolved issues (if any) do you have about the husband-wife relationship?

Imagine you are a parent writing a note to your son or daughter before his/her wedding day. Reflecting on the above verses, what is one thing you would write about being a godly husband or wife?

DIVORCE

The sad reality is that more than half of American couples will probably end up getting divorced. Sometimes it's easier to change our spouses than to change ourselves. Whether or not you are currently married, you are being influenced by the marriages — and the divorces — happening around you.

How has divorce (experienced directly or indirectly) affected you?

In these passages, mark and write on the chart below what they say about marriage and divorce.

MALACHI 2:14-16. You cry out, "Why doesn't the LORD accept my worship?" I'll tell you why! Because the LORD witnessed the vows you and your wife made when you were young. But you have been unfaithful to her, though she remained your faithful partner, the wife of your marriage vows.

Didn't the LORD make you one with your wife? In body and spirit you are his. And what does he want? Godly children from your union. So guard your heart; remain loyal to the wife of your youth. "For I hate divorce!" says the LORD, the God of Israel. "To divorce your wife is to overwhelm her with cruelty," says the LORD of Heaven's Armies. (NLT)

MATTHEW 19:3-12. Some Pharisees came and tried to trap him with this question: "Should a man be allowed to divorce his wife for just any reason?"

"Haven't you read the Scriptures?" Jesus replied. "They record that from the beginning 'God made them male and female.' And he said, 'This explains why a man leaves his father and mother and is joined to his wife, and the two are united into one.' Since they are no longer two but one, let no one split apart what God has joined together."

"Then why did Moses say in the law that a man could give his wife a written notice of divorce and send her away?" they asked.

Jesus replied, "Moses permitted divorce only as a concession to your hard hearts, but it was not what God had originally intended. And I tell you this, whoever divorces his wife and marries someone else commits adultery — unless his wife has been unfaithful."

Jesus' disciples then said to him, "If this is the case, it is better not to marry!"

"Not everyone can accept this statement," Jesus said. "Only those whom God helps. Some are born as eunuchs, some have been made eunuchs by others, and some choose not to marry for the sake of the Kingdom of Heaven. Let anyone accept this who can." (NLT)

From these passages, summarize God's perspective on marriage and divorce.

MARRIAGE	DIVORCE

If you've been divorced, how has God met you in the midst of your relational pains? If you have never been divorced, how can you offer grace and support to a divorced friend?

Has God brought any healthy, Christ-centered married couples into your life who have (or could) give you hope for your future marriage and family? Describe them. If not, we urge you to seek them out.

PRAYER PAUSE

No matter what your family background — healthy, broken, married, divorced, adopted, or abandoned — in Christ you are adopted into the family of God and chosen to be Christ's bride. As you reflect on what it means to be in a family, take some time to tell God your experience of being adopted into His family. Imagine your future inheritance. Afterward ask the Holy Spirit as the Comforter to bring healing into your earthly family if needed.

PAUSE 4_JOURNEYING FORWARD

1 JOHN 4:10-11. This is love: not that we loved God, but that he loved us. . . . Dear friends, since God so loved us, we also ought to love one another.

Select one verse or passage that was meaningful to you this week and write it here.

We live in a world of images that deeply influence how we look at life. Choose a picture from this chapter that is meaningful or disturbing to you, and briefly explain why.

How have you experienced God this week?

Reflecting on what was most meaningful to you from this chapter, respond to one (or more) of these questions in the Journal on the following page:

- What impact does the loving way of Jesus have on your heart?
- As you and your friends love one another, how might you all be helping others see God and His love?
- What one action step are you motivated to take in response to what God has taught you?

JOURNAL

SUGGESTED MEMORY VERSE:

LOVING IN FAMILIES — PSALM 68:5-6, NLT

Father to the fatherless, defender of widows — this is God, whose dwelling is holy. God places the lonely in families.

DIGGING DEEPER_ON PARENTS AND CHILDREN

The Bible challenges parents to raise their children with love, faith, and hope. No parents on earth ever do this perfectly. God is the only perfect parent. So please don't allow this exercise to make you critical or use it to show your parents where they may have missed the boat. Instead, use it as a framework to help you reflect on how you were parented, or to envision yourself as a parent someday, or to be a better parent now — either practically or spiritually.

Please rate the following statements using this scale:

1. NO, I don't feel this way.
2. I SELDOM feel this way.
3. I feel this way SOMETIMES.
4. I USUALLY feel this way.
5. YES, I STRONGLY feel this way.

BUILDING SECURITY THROUGH LOVE:

Dad	Mom	(If Dad and Mom were not your primary caregivers, write the names of those who were.)
____	____	WANTED me not only for what I did but also for who I was.
____	____	FORGAVE and ACCEPTED me when I was wrong.
____	____	WELCOMED me being with him/her.
____	____	ENCOURAGED (CHEERED) me when I was troubled or discouraged.
____	____	Appropriately gave me physical TOUCHES (hugs but without sexual overtures).
____	____	COMFORTED me when I was in pain, affirmed that the pain was okay, offered to help me.
____	____	CARRIED me (intervened and protected me) when I was over my head in a situation.
____	____	KEPT his/her promises to me.
____	____	DIRECTED me to rely on God for love and acceptance.
____	____	MODELED going to God for love and acceptance.
____	____	TOTALS (The higher the score, the better for building security in a child.)

BUILDING STRENGTH THROUGH FAITH:

Dad	Mom	
____	____	BELIEVED in me as I matured even though I sometimes acted immaturely.
____	____	Saw my potential and SUPPORTED me in reaching it.
____	____	FREED me to be and do differently from him/her.
____	____	Helped me DEVELOP according to my strengths and abilities.
____	____	ALLOWED me to make my own decisions when appropriate.
____	____	Helped DISCIPLINE me to learn self-discipline.
____	____	INSTILLED in me courage to be honest, humble, and to do good.
____	____	CREATED SAFETY so I could learn to trust.
____	____	TAUGHT me to rely on God for my strength.
____	____	MODELED getting his/her strength from God.
____	____	TOTALS (The higher the score, the better for building strength in a child.)

BUILDING MEANING & PURPOSE THROUGH HOPE:

Dad	Mom	
____	____	APPRECIATED me as a unique and special person.
____	____	RESPECTED me for who I was.
____	____	HONORED me (didn't invade my personal space or demand to know all my secrets).
____	____	EXHORTED me to do what is morally good.
____	____	ACKNOWLEDGED and was proud of my accomplishments.
____	____	Freely RECEIVED my love for him/her.
____	____	ENCOURAGED me to believe that I could make a difference in the world.
____	____	HELPED me prepare for the future.
____	____	TAUGHT me to rely on God for my purpose and meaning in life.
____	____	MODELED getting his/her sense of meaning and purpose from God.
____	____	TOTALS (The higher the score, the better for building meaning and purpose in a child.)

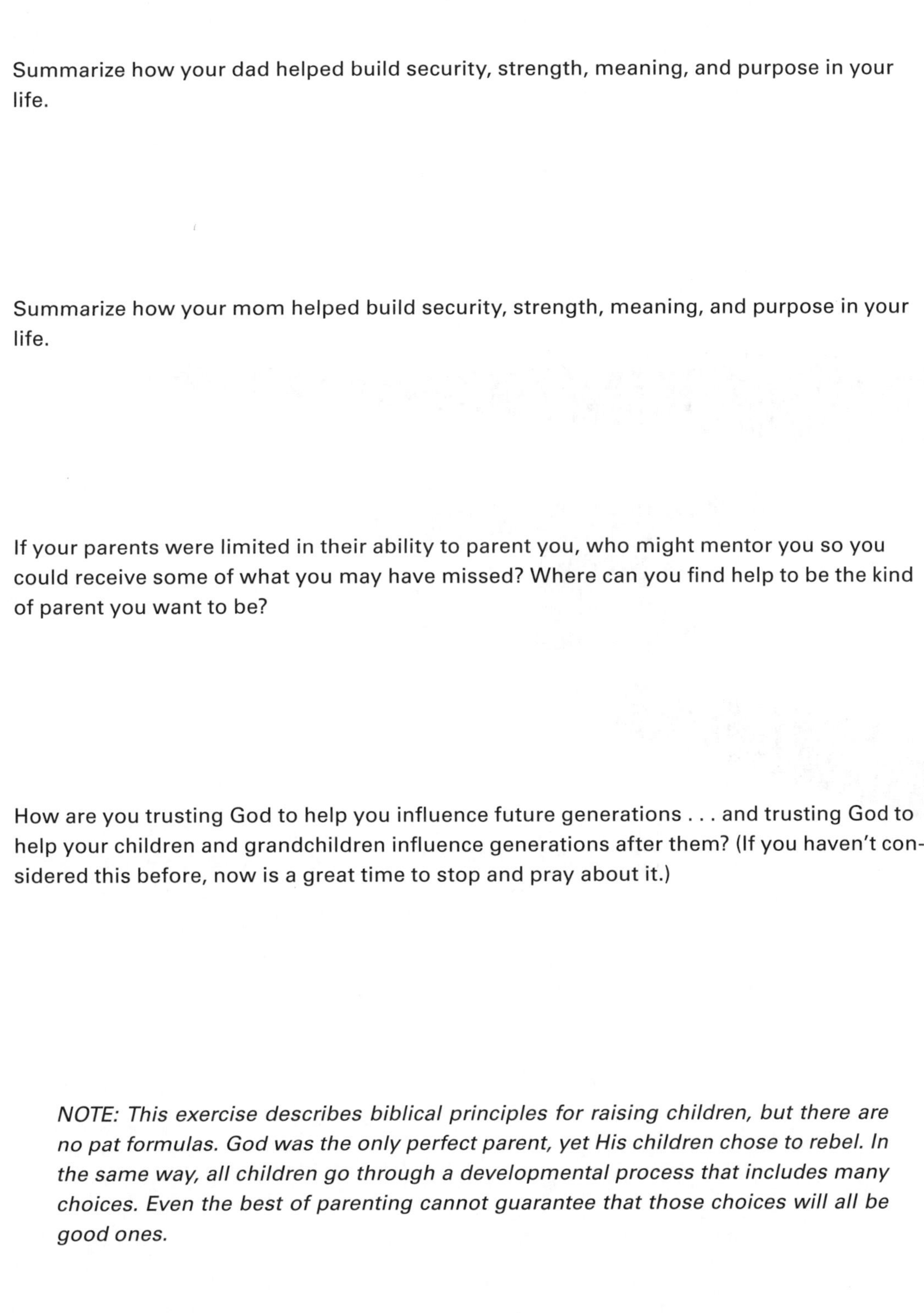

Summarize how your dad helped build security, strength, meaning, and purpose in your life.

Summarize how your mom helped build security, strength, meaning, and purpose in your life.

If your parents were limited in their ability to parent you, who might mentor you so you could receive some of what you may have missed? Where can you find help to be the kind of parent you want to be?

How are you trusting God to help you influence future generations . . . and trusting God to help your children and grandchildren influence generations after them? (If you haven't considered this before, now is a great time to stop and pray about it.)

NOTE: This exercise describes biblical principles for raising children, but there are no pat formulas. God was the only perfect parent, yet His children chose to rebel. In the same way, all children go through a developmental process that includes many choices. Even the best of parenting cannot guarantee that those choices will all be good ones.

CHAPTER 5
LOVING FRIENDS

Jessica has a lot of friends. People greet her everywhere she goes — work, her apartment building, church, and even the grocery store. She gets so many calls on her cell phone that she assigned a different ring tone for each circle of friends. These circles of friends have become family for Jessica. After work hours they gather at a coffee shop. Talk is good. This is what life is really about. Friends.

But when she gets home — especially at night — she still feels unknown and lonely. Usually Jessica appreciates her friends. But every once in a while the inevitable happens: someone breaks a confidence and shares private information with someone else. This always plays out badly. People find out. People get hurt. Revenge sometimes occurs.

Jessica doesn't know who to trust and who not to trust. So she tends to keep everybody at a safe distance from what's really going on in her life. Friends and friendships are very important to Jessica, but she doesn't really feel "known." She wonders if others feel this way too. Secretly Jessica desires a few close friends but is afraid it might not be worth the risk.

At one point Jesus tells His disciples, "I no longer call you servants, because a servant does not know his master's business. Instead, I have called you friends, for everything that I learned from my Father I have made known to you" (John 15:15). Jesus was interested in sustaining His friends more than He was in promoting Himself.

— ALAN ANDREWS AND CHRISTOPHER MORTON

What part of Jessica's story (if any) can you relate to?

Do you know someone like Jessica? *Explain.*

PAUSE 1_EXPLORING WHAT GOD SAYS

In our fast-paced society, many of us are in contact with lots of people through e-mail, in the classroom, at the fitness center, at work, at church, and in our neighborhoods. Maybe you're lucky enough to be blessed with several good friends. But the reality for many of us is that we're busy — but still lonely. We're active — but not really known. We're in constant contact with people, but we may not feel very connected. Many of us long for a sense of being known in community with others. Building deep friendships takes time, work, and energy. But good friends are among God's most wonderful gifts and life's greatest treasures.

In these verses, circle or highlight what you learn about the value of friends.

> *HEBREWS 10:24-25. And let us consider how we may spur one another on toward love and good deeds. Let us not give up meeting together, as some are in the habit of doing, but let us encourage one another — and all the more as you see the Day approaching.*
>
> *ECCLESIASTES 4:9-12. Two are better than one, because they have a good return for their work: If one falls down, his friend can help him up. But pity the man who falls and has no one to help him up! Also, if two lie down together, they will keep warm. But how can one keep warm alone? Though one may be overpowered, two can defend themselves. A cord of three strands is not quickly broken.*
>
> *PROVERBS 27:17. As iron sharpens iron, so a friend sharpens a friend.* (NLT)

When has one of your friends helped you in a way mentioned above?

Everyone needs some good friends. But some "friends" aren't really good friends. If you want to know how to choose a good, trustworthy, safe friend — and how to be such a friend — the book of Proverbs is packed with wisdom about expressing love in practical ways, especially to friends. Study the verses in the following chart.

Left column: Summarize what you notice about the behavior and influence of a trustworthy friend.

Right column: Summarize what you notice about the behavior and influence of an untrustworthy friend.

A TRUSTWORTHY FRIEND	PROVERBS (ALL FROM NLT)	AN UNTRUSTWORTHY FRIEND
Wise, gentle friend . . . Enjoys learning Gets along well	PROVERBS 15:1-2. A gentle answer deflects anger, but harsh words make tempers flare. The tongue of the wise makes knowledge appealing, but the mouth of a fool belches out foolishness.	Harsh, foolish friend . . . Stirs up conflict Talks trash
Trustworthy friend . . . Keeps what I share confidential	PROVERBS 11:13. A gossip goes around telling secrets, but those who are trustworthy can keep a confidence.	Gossipy friend . . .
Wise friend . . .	PROVERBS 12:22-23. The Lord detests lying lips, but he delights in those who tell the truth. The wise don't make a show of their knowledge, but fools broadcast their foolishness.	Foolish friend . . .
Godly friend . . .	PROVERBS 14:9. Fools make fun of guilt, but the godly acknowledge it and seek reconciliation.	Foolish friend . . .
Cool-tempered friend . . .	PROVERBS 15:18. A hot-tempered person starts fights; a cool-tempered person stops them.	Hot-headed friend . . .
Understanding friend . . .	PROVERBS 18:2. Fools have no interest in understanding; they only want to air their own opinions.	Foolish friend . . .
Real friend . . .	PROVERBS 18:24. There are "friends" who destroy each other, but a real friend sticks closer than a brother.	"Friend" . . .
True friend . . .	PROVERBS 27:6. Wounds from a sincere friend are better than many kisses from an enemy.	Enemy . . .

Select one proverb from the list that describes an experience you have had with a friend. Summarize it below.

> EXAMPLE: Proverbs 27:6 Jake tried to warn me that I was treating my girlfriend like dirt. Sure, it hurt. But he was a better friend than Todd who was calling her up all the time when he was supposed to be my friend.
>
> YOUR EXAMPLE:

One all-too-common kind of untrustworthy friend is described in this verse:

> *PROVERBS 26:18-19. Just as damaging as a madman shooting a deadly weapon is someone who lies to a friend and then says, "I was only joking."* (NLT)

Describe a time when you have been hurt by a friend's sarcasm or joking. Or describe a time when you hurt someone with your own sarcasm or joking.

In what areas are you a safe and trustworthy friend? In what areas might you need to grow to become a better friend?

Sarcasm: a verbal "knife" disguised as humor.

PAUSE 2_EXPLORING YOUR REALITY

Mother Teresa once was asked about the worst disease she had ever seen. Was it leprosy or smallpox? Was it AIDS or Alzheimer's? "No," she said, "the worst disease I've ever seen is loneliness."

— LEONARD SWEET, *OUT OF THE QUESTION . . . INTO THE MYSTERY*

How lonely have you felt in the last year or two? (Mark the arrow and explain below.)

ISOLATED, DESPERATELY LONELY . . . BUSY WITH PEOPLE BUT UNKNOWN . . . WELL-CONNECTED AND KNOWN

Out of the many — or few — people you consider friends, who do you trust with the real you? Why?

Think about who your close friends are. What needs do you wish your friends would meet in your life?

How are you doing at meeting some needs of your friends? *Explain.*

If you have moved from place to place, how has this affected your friendships?

In the opening story, Jessica's friends "had become family" to her. Do you view any of your family members as your close friends? *Explain.*

FRIENDSHIP ASSESSMENT

It is life-changing to have a few friends who know you inside and out — and still love you! But it just isn't practical or wise to have a vulnerable, intimate relationship with all your friends. Think about someone you regard as a close friend. Write his/her initials here: _________ . Do this exercise to identify areas where you already know each other well, along with areas where one or both of you might want to go deeper.

Rate each item on a scale of 1-5 (1=low, 5=high).

I SHARE THIS WITH MY FRIEND	AREAS OF OUR LIVES	MY FRIEND SHARES THIS WITH ME
	Facts about life — past and present	
	Daily joys and irritations	
	Family issues	
	Opinions on current events and trends	
	Significant pains from the past	
	Important accomplishments	
	Fears, struggles, and disappointments	
	Desires and ambitions	
	Where we are with God or spiritual journey	
	Financial, sexual, shameful, or emotional struggles	

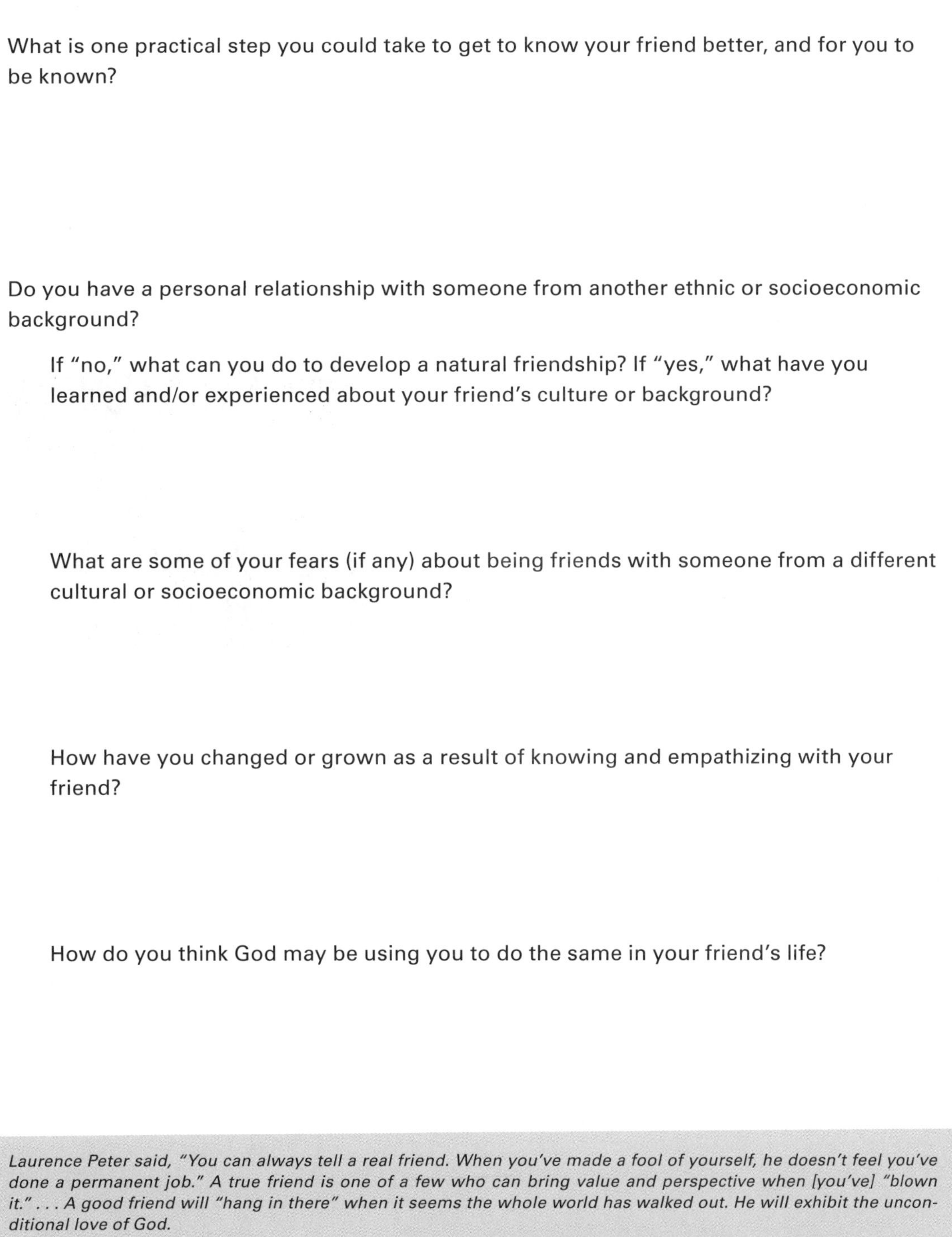

What is one practical step you could take to get to know your friend better, and for you to be known?

Do you have a personal relationship with someone from another ethnic or socioeconomic background?

If "no," what can you do to develop a natural friendship? If "yes," what have you learned and/or experienced about your friend's culture or background?

What are some of your fears (if any) about being friends with someone from a different cultural or socioeconomic background?

How have you changed or grown as a result of knowing and empathizing with your friend?

How do you think God may be using you to do the same in your friend's life?

Laurence Peter said, "You can always tell a real friend. When you've made a fool of yourself, he doesn't feel you've done a permanent job." A true friend is one of a few who can bring value and perspective when [you've] "blown it." . . . A good friend will "hang in there" when it seems the whole world has walked out. He will exhibit the unconditional love of God.

— DENNIS AND BARBARA RAINEY, *BUILDING YOUR MATE'S SELF-ESTEEM*

PAUSE 3_COMING ALIVE TO GOD AND OTHERS

BACKGROUND

David's closest friend was Jonathan, the first-born son and heir apparent to King Saul of Israel. Jonathan knew, however, that David was God's choice as the future king, not Jonathan. Despite Saul's insecurities and murderous plots against David, the two friends remained loyally committed to each other through years of testing. They show us what it means to trust each other with themselves.

CASE STUDY IN FRIENDSHIP:

DAVID AND JONATHAN

In the last chapter, we studied the not-so-perfect family life of David. Despite the pain in David's various families and relational networks, he was blessed with many quality friends whose influence on him contributed greatly to his being "a man after God's heart."

As you read the story of their lifelong relationship, make observations about what it takes to build and protect a quality friendship. After reading each scene, write some observations about what made their friendship so good.

SCENE 1: Making a Friend

Read 1 SAMUEL 18:1-4. Write your observations about making and being a quality friend:

SCENE 2: Defending/Standing Up for a Friend

Read 1 SAMUEL 19:1-7. Write your observations about defending and standing up for a friend:

SCENE 3: Protecting a Friend

Read 1 SAMUEL 20 (especially verses 1-4,11-17,30-34,41-42). Write your observations about protecting a friend:

SCENE 4: Encouraging and Affirming a Friend

> *1 SAMUEL 23:16-18. Jonathan, Saul's son, visited David at Horesh and encouraged him [strengthened his hand — RSV] in God. He said, "Don't despair. My father, Saul, can't lay a hand on you. You will be Israel's king and I'll be right at your side to help. And my father knows it." Then the two of them made a covenant before GOD. David stayed at Horesh and Jonathan went home.* (MSG)

Your observations about encouraging and affirming a friend:

What qualities of friendship from David and Jonathan's relationship do you want to see in your own life?

When was a time someone encouraged you to remember God's promises for your life?

[May] God make us all His Jonathans. . . . Notice what [Jonathan] does: he does not so comfort David that he becomes necessary to him. "He strengthened his hand in God." He leaves his friend strong in God, resting in God, safe in God. He [separates] his dear David from himself and attaches him to God. . . . If David had leaned on Jonathan, if Jonathan had made himself necessary to David, David would not have learned to lean on his Rock and proved the glorious strength of his Rock; his whole life would have been lived on a lower level. . . . So let us not weaken those whom we love with weak sympathy, but let us love them enough to [separate] them from ourselves and strengthen their hands in God.

— AMY CARMICHAEL, *EDGES OF HIS WAYS*

Who is a "Jonathan" to you? Who looks to you as a "Jonathan"? *Explain.*

Is there a friend who has become too dependent on you and not dependent enough on God and others? What can you do to "strengthen his/her hand in God"?

PRAYER PAUSE

Talk with Jesus about your friendship with Him. Thank Him for His friendship love that moved Him to lay down His life for you. Enjoy unhurried time with the One known as "the friend of sinners."

DEEPENING FRIENDSHIPS

AFFIRMING ONE ANOTHER

One way to deepen friendship is to affirm what is good and true about each other. It is important to affirm your friends' character and who they are, not just what they do. In your discussion group, choose one of the following ways to do that:

1. IN WRITING: Each group member writes his/her own name at the bottom of a sheet of paper. Pass it to the right. Then take a few minutes to write 2-3 sentences at the top, affirming the person whose name is on the sheet — such as what you like or appreciate, strengths, etc. When you are done, fold the paper over to cover your comments, leaving the person's name exposed at the bottom. Pass the sheets around until everyone has written something affirming or encouraging about everyone else.
2. IN THE WHOLE GROUP: All group members will share what they appreciate about one group member. Then take turns until everyone has affirmed everyone else. Ask one person in the group to take notes on what is affirmed, so each person can take away a record of this time of affirmation.
3. IN PAIRS: One way is to break into pairs and share.

DOING ACTIVITIES AND SERVING TOGETHER

Friendships often are developed by doing favorite activities together, such as music or sports. Who can you invite to join you in an activity this week?

Serving together is another way to deepen friendships and experience life on a different level. For example, you might serve meals to the homeless, visit the elderly, work on a home building project, or take action on a global issue. How could you and some friends or your group serve others together?

Most men don't have friendships beyond a surface level. What's worse is they don't know how to deepen them. . . . Men are more inclined to find the added significance a friend provides in pursuits such as business, politics or sports.

— DENNIS AND BARBARA RAINEY, *BUILDING YOUR MATE'S SELF-ESTEEM*

MAKING LIFE CHANGES TOGETHER

Another way to deepen friendships is to accomplish purposeful life changes together. To get started:

- Think about the future . . . share your dreams or ambitions.
- Think about life today . . . share a significant change you would like to make during the next six months (perhaps develop more friendships, date more frequently, lose weight, change jobs, seek God in a new way, restore a relationship).
- Share what you will start doing or do differently in order to reach your goals.
- Share what obstacles might prevent you from being successful in making these changes.
- Believe God together. Ask the Holy Spirit to empower you as you seek to change.
- Decide how your friends can support you and how you will stay connected in the next six months.

Consider choosing one of the above activities and come prepared to tell your group about it next week.

PAUSE 4_JOURNEYING FORWARD

1 JOHN 4:10-11. This is love: not that we loved God, but that he loved us. . . . Dear friends, since God so loved us, we also ought to love one another.

Select one verse or passage that was meaningful to you this week and write it here.

We live in a world of images that deeply influence how we look at life. Choose a picture from this chapter that is meaningful or disturbing to you, and briefly explain why.

How have you experienced God this week?

Reflecting on what was most meaningful to you from this chapter, respond to one (or more) of these questions in the Journal on the following page:

- What impact does the loving way of Jesus have on your heart?
- As you and your friends love one another, how might you all be helping others see God and His love?
- What one action step are you motivated to take in response to what God has taught you?

JOURNAL

SUGGESTED MEMORY VERSE:

LOVING FRIENDS — PROVERBS 18:24, NLT

There are "friends" who destroy each other, but a real friend sticks closer than a brother.

DIGGING DEEPER

CASE STUDY: NATHAN — A FRIEND AS TRUTH-TELLER

Besides Jonathan, God sent David another friend to help him through a critical time of moral failure and personal crisis: the prophet Nathan. Read about their relationship in these passages:

Read 2 SAMUEL 7:1-17. Write your observations about a friend who confronts in love.

Read 2 SAMUEL 12:1-14 and 24-25. Write your observations about a friend who brings encouragement and hope.

How did the Holy Spirit use Nathan to "speak the truth in love" to David when he needed it? (Ephesians 4:15)

Who (if anyone) among your friends has been like a "Nathan" to you? How did he/she help you?

Do you have a friend whom you could love by speaking the truth to them? If so, how can you deliver your message with kindness that leads to repentance? (Romans 2:4)

CHAPTER 6
LOVING PEOPLE DIFFERENT FROM ME

When Tina first met the new family on the block, she couldn't figure them out. First there was Terrell, about twenty, probably biracial, with some pretty wild tattoos and body-piercing. Then there was an old lady — an old white lady. She kinda shuffled around with her walker and seemed confused most of the time, and she was obsessive about all her cats. From such different worlds, Tina wondered how those two could possibly connect?

Then one day Tina stopped by their house to return one of the cats that had crept into her garage. The living room was crammed with pictures of Terrell as a baby, as a child, as a teenager. The old lady smiled sweetly and said, "You've met my grandson Terrell, haven't you? He's such a great help to me with his mom in a treatment center, and his dad, well, he's not around. It's just the two of us. But somehow the good Lord helps us get through each day."

That explained the affection she saw between them. Those two were separated by age and race and a dozen other differences. But somehow love brought them together.

When was a time that you were loved by (or had a positive experience with) someone different from you — someone who loved you through your differences?

What happened in your lives as a result?

We've probably all said or felt it sometime or other. *They* are different. *They* are inferior. *They* act superior. *They* have too much power. Whatever words we use, it all usually boils down to *they* are not like *me*. The telltale pronoun of intolerance is *they*. How much hurt has been caused in this world because we have trouble getting along with people different from ourselves? People different from us in nationality, in race or ethnic group, in gender, in social or financial standing, in religion — in a hundred other ways. But what if we changed the pronoun to *we*? We are different. We are not like each other — and that is good. We come in lots of different flavors — and those differences can enrich us all instead of divide us. Or better yet — "I am different — just as we all are!"

When we love people who are different from us, we're taking a risk — just as Jesus took a huge risk when He lived among, loved, and died for people who were so different from Him. Like Jesus, we're called to move from harmless indifference into intentional engagement. That never happens without setting aside pride and embracing humility. In this journey of loving the diverse people around us, Jesus is our model. In this chapter we'll take a look at how Jesus loved others — especially those different from Him.

How I treat my brothers and sisters from day to day, whether they are Caucasian, African, Asian, or Hispanic; how I react to the sin-scarred wino on the street; how I respond to interruptions from people I dislike; how I deal with ordinary people in their ordinary unbelief on an ordinary day will speak the truth of who I am more poignantly than the pro-life sticker on the bumper of my car.

— ROBERT J. WICKS, *TOUCHING THE HOLY*

PAUSE 1_EXPLORING WHAT GOD SAYS

CELEBRATING DIVERSITY IN HEAVEN

Have you ever taken a diversity seminar on campus or at your workplace? Whatever reasons were presented for celebrating diversity, here's an even better one. In heaven there won't be any hostility between different races or ethnic groups or between the poor and the rich. Picture this scene from heaven as shown to John in a vision:

> *REVELATION 7:9-10,16-17. After this I looked and there before me was a great multitude that no one could count, from every nation, tribe, people and language, standing before the throne and in front of the Lamb. They were wearing white robes and were holding palm branches in their hands. And they cried out in a loud voice:*

> *"Salvation belongs to our God, who sits on the throne, and to the Lamb." . . .*
>
> *Never again will they hunger; never again will they thirst. The sun will not beat upon them, nor any scorching heat. For the Lamb at the center of the throne will be their shepherd; he will lead them to springs of living water. And God will wipe away every tear from their eyes.*

Who will be in the crowd worshipping before the throne of Christ in heaven?

What has the Lamb promised to do for them?

That is the picture God has given us of what it will be like in heaven. So how do you think God feels about the diversity among human beings on earth? How do you feel?

JESUS AND THE LEPER

Jesus came to reconcile God and humanity and bring us into His Father's kingdom. And He also came to reconcile people separated by all kinds of barriers. He came so we might truly "love others as ourselves" regardless of race, religion, or any other difference. In Jesus' society, as in ours, some people were considered "different" from the rest. Notice how in each case, people knew they were loved because Jesus' compassion gave them dignity.

HISTORICAL BACKGROUND ON LEPERS

In Bible times the various diseases called "leprosy" were greatly feared and highly contagious. The worst form slowly ruined the body and, in most cases, was fatal. Religious law required lepers to live away from their families and friends, outside the towns, because they were considered "unclean"—and therefore unfit to participate in religious or social activities. People believed they would become unclean if they touched a leper, so some people threw rocks at lepers to keep them at a safe distance. Rabbis and priests were especially careful to avoid lepers, or else they couldn't perform their religious duties. (Adapted from The Application Bible, *World Bible Publishers, Inc., 1988.)*

Read MARK 1:40-45 about one of Jesus' encounters with a person suffering from leprosy. What did Jesus do in response to the leper's request?

How do you think Jesus' compassion made the leper feel?

What do you think it cost Jesus to love this social "outsider" (verse 45)?

Sometimes lepers were considered as "outcasts" and "untouchables." Although it varies from place to place, every society still has its social outcasts. Maybe today it's the disabled, the AIDS victims, the homeless, or immigrants.

WHO ARE THE "OUTCASTS" OR "UNTOUCHABLES" IN OUR SOCIETY? (Groups)	**WHO ARE THE "OUTCASTS" IN YOUR CONTEXT? (Individuals)**

JESUS AND THE SAMARITAN WOMAN

HISTORICAL BACKGROUND

The Samaritans were a racially mixed society—what we might call "half-breeds." The religion they practiced was also considered pagan. By the time of Christ, most Jews despised Samaritans and excluded them from their homes and religious activities. To avoid being "contaminated" by contact with Samaritans, Jews used to go miles out of their way rather than travel through Samaria. The typical Jewish man's attitude toward women back then wasn't much better than his attitude toward Samaritans. He probably started the day thanking God that he wasn't created a Gentile, a slave, or a woman!

(ADAPTED FROM WWW.BIBLE-HISTORY.COM AND WWW.CHRISTIANCOURIER.COM.)

Read JOHN 4:27-30,34-42. It reveals how Jesus loved someone different from Him in race, ethnic background, religion, gender, social status, and of questionable character.

Both the woman (verse 9) and the disciples (verse 27) were astonished that Jesus was having a conversation with her. How do you think Jesus was able to overcome the cultural taboo against a Jewish man associating with a Samaritan, a woman, and an adulterer?

By ignoring several traditional "walls of hostility," how did Jesus' love impact . . .

. . . THIS WOMAN?	. . . HER COMMUNITY?
. . . HIS DISCIPLES?	. . . US?

Who are the counterparts to the Samaritan woman . . .

. . . today in our society (think of groups of people):

. . . in your particular context (think of individuals):

From Jesus' example, what are some practical ways that you can begin to demonstrate Jesus' love to people of another religion, ethnic, or socioeconomic background?

Remember that *you* are *they* to somebody — you make them uncomfortable because you're different. Has anyone ever treated you like an "outcast" or "untouchable" or a "Samaritan woman"? *Explain*.

PRAYER PAUSE

Can you remember a time when you were hurt or marginalized as a result of being different from others? Or a time when you may have hurt or marginalized someone else because they were different from you? In either case, pause to talk it over with God. Allow God's mercy and grace to be with you in that place. Journal your prayer time here . . .

PAUSE 2_EXPLORING YOUR REALITY

In Jesus' daily reality, there was serious religious and cultural hostility dividing the Jews and the Gentiles (non-Jews). Jesus came to break down "[destroy, abolish] the hostile dividing wall" between them (Ephesians 2:14, AMP).

> *EPHESIANS 2:14. For He is [Himself] our peace (our bond of unity and harmony). He has made us both [Jew and Gentile] one [body], and has broken down (destroyed, abolished) the hostile dividing wall between us.* (AMP)

By placing His kingdom in our hands, Jesus calls us to do the same thing: break down whatever walls of hostility are dividing people around the world and in our neighborhoods. Take a few minutes to think of groups of people around the world who are currently (or were historically) divided by walls of hostility. Write them on opposite sides of this wall.

EXAMPLES:

Jews in Europe
Hutus in Rwanda

Nazis
Tutsis

Now take a minute to think more locally and in your environments about people or groups divided by hostility. Write them on opposite sides of this wall.

Jocks in high school
Landlords

Nerds
Renters / tenants

What do you think are some consequences of not loving people different from us — globally and locally?

We all have different comfort levels when it comes to being with people who are different from us. Study the list below highlighting some ways people are different from one another.

Circle any difference that tends to make you uncomfortable. Be real!

- Race
- Gender
- Mental capacity
- Physical capacity
- Age
- Legal standing
- Moral habits
- Personality
- Economic status
- Physical appearance
- Clothing style
- Religious orientation
- Sexual orientation or habits
- Social status
- Health or fitness
- Other differences? ______________________________

Now underline any that you were surprised to sense in yourself.

Now go a little deeper into your emotions. Why do you think you have felt uncomfortable or unloving around people with these differences? Was it:

____ ignorance
____ fear
____ embarrassment
____ perceived threat
____ feeling helpless
____ guilt
____ stereotype or prejudice from your peers, family, culture, or media
____ you were hurt by someone like them in the past
____ others? ____________________

How does walking in the Spirit of God help us relate in a healthy way to people different from us?

When God brings somebody into your life who is different from you, who makes you feel uncomfortable, how will you communicate dignity and respond in love?

Think of a time when you had a positive experience with someone different from you — someone who loved you through your differences. Consider contacting that person to express what that meant to you. Or bring a picture, story, poem, or song that celebrates "loving through differences" to share with your group.

PAUSE 3_COMING ALIVE TO GOD AND OTHERS

The exclusion of the weak and insignificant, the seemingly useless people, from a Christian community may actually mean the exclusion of Christ; in the poor brother Christ is knocking at the door.

— DIETRICH BONHOEFFER

GOD'S HEART FOR THE POOR

There is one group of people that God seems to have special compassion for — the poor and oppressed. There are more than 175 passages in the Bible regarding the poor. He wants us to partner with Him by helping those poorer than we are in material resources. As you read these passages:

- Highlight some ways to show love and respect to the poor and oppressed among us.
- For each passage, write in the margin one practical way you could put it into practice.

PRACTICAL APPLICATION

LEVITICUS 23:22. When you reap the harvest of your land, do not reap to the very edges of your field or gather the gleanings of your harvest. Leave them for the poor and the alien. I am the L*ORD your God.*

Take my usable extra stuff to the re-sale store instead of tossing it out.

PSALM 82:3-4. Give justice to the poor and the orphan; uphold the rights of the oppressed and the destitute. Rescue the poor and helpless; deliver them from the grasp of evil people. (NLT)

LUKE 6:38. Give, and it will be given to you. A good measure, pressed down, shaken together and running over, will be poured into your lap. For with the measure you use, it will be measured to you.

ISAIAH 58:6-7,10. Is not this the kind of fasting I have chosen: to loose the chains of injustice and untie the cords of the yoke, to set the oppressed free and break every yoke? Is it not to share your food with the hungry and to provide the poor wanderer with shelter — when you see the naked, to clothe him, and not to turn away from your own flesh and blood? . . . And if you spend yourselves in behalf of the hungry and satisfy the needs of the oppressed, then your light will rise in the darkness, and your night will become like the noonday.

Have you seen or experienced anything that has made you sensitive to poverty or to social or racial injustice in the world? *Explain.*

What opportunities have you had or what work have you done to express your practical desire for mercy and justice? How were you blessed?

As you read this passage, imagine how it would feel to be treated like the poor person.

> *JAMES 2:1-4. My dear brothers and sisters, how can you claim to have faith in our glorious Lord Jesus Christ if you favor some people over others? For example, suppose someone comes into your meeting dressed in fancy clothes and expensive jewelry, and another comes in who is poor and dressed in dirty clothes. If you give special attention and a good seat to the rich person, but you say to the poor one, "You can stand over there, or else sit on the floor" — well, doesn't this discrimination show that your judgments are guided by evil motives?* (NLT)

Think of a time when you did not receive "the good seat." How would or does it feel to live your life being discriminated against?

If you see someone being treated with discrimination, what are your options for responding?

Do we look at the poor with compassion? They are hungry not only for food, they are hungry to be recognized as human beings. They are hungry for dignity and to be treated as we are treated. They are hungry for our love.

— MOTHER TERESA, *A SIMPLE PATH*

Consider these verses on the pros and cons of wealth and poverty.

> *JAMES 2:5. Listen, my dear brothers: Has not God chosen those who are poor in the eyes of the world to be rich in faith and to inherit the kingdom he promised those who love him?*
>
> *REVELATION 3:17. You say, "I am rich; I have acquired wealth and do not need a thing." But you do not realize that you are wretched, pitiful, poor, blind and naked.*

What do the "rich" need from others that money can't buy? What riches do the "poor" have to offer?

When we help the poor and oppressed, how might we also be "overcoming evil with good" (Romans 12:21) and revealing God's love?

APPLICATION OPPORTUNITY

Respecting the dignity of every individual through love involves coming alongside them to communicate support, confidence, and respect — all of which opens up important new relationships.

— EDDIE BROUSSARD, "ENVIRONMENTS OF GRACE AND TRUTH"

Ask God if, why, and how you should come alongside someone who is different from you with practical love and assistance. Then write down your first step of action.

- HOW could you begin to show love in a tangible way while still respecting dignity?
- WHAT specific little initiatives could you take to reach across your differences?
- HOW might you take these initiatives in partnership with others, not just by yourself?
- WHAT would it cost you to love people who are different from you?

CELEBRATING DIFFERENCES ON EARTH

Consider what Christ has done to bring together people who were once divided by their differences.

(NOTE: Jews referred to anyone who wasn't a Jew as a "Gentile.")

GALATIANS 3:26-28. You are all sons of God through faith in Christ Jesus, for all of you who were baptized into Christ have clothed yourselves with Christ. There is neither Jew nor Greek, slave nor free, male nor female, for you are all one in Christ Jesus.

EPHESIANS 2:14-19. For Christ himself has brought peace to us. He united Jews and Gentiles into one people when, in his own body on the cross, he broke down the wall of hostility that separated us. He did this by ending the system of law with its commandments and regulations. He made peace between Jews and Gentiles by creating in himself one new people from the two groups. Together as one body, Christ reconciled both groups to God by means of his death on the cross, and our hostility toward each other was put to death. He brought this Good News of peace to you Gentiles who were far away from him, and peace to the Jews who were near. Now all of us can come to the Father through the same Holy Spirit because of what Christ has done for us. So now you Gentiles are no longer strangers and foreigners. You are citizens along with all of God's holy people. You are members of God's family. (NLT)

From these passages, what did Jesus do to "[kill] the mutual enmity and [bring] the feud to an end" (Ephesians 2:16, AMP) among people separated and hostile because of their differences?

How has this study motivated you to respect and celebrate diversity and move forward in relationships with people who are different from you?

CLOSING PRAYER

(Consider praying this aloud with your group.)

O GOD, who created all peoples in your image, we thank you for the wonderful diversity of races and cultures in this world. Enrich our lives by ever-widening circles of fellowship, and show us your presence in those who differ most from us, until our knowledge of your love is made perfect in our love for all your children, through Jesus Christ our Lord. Amen.

— The Book of Common Prayer[1]

[1] Thanksgivings, #7, *The Book of Common Prayer* (New Jersey: The Seabury Press, 1979), 840.

PAUSE 4_JOURNEYING FORWARD

> *1 JOHN 4:10-11. This is love: not that we loved God, but that he loved us. . . . Dear friends, since God so loved us, we also ought to love one another.*

Select one verse or passage that was meaningful to you this week and write it here.

We live in a world of images that deeply influence how we look at life. Choose a picture from this chapter that is meaningful or disturbing to you, and briefly explain why.

How have you experienced God this week?

Reflecting on what was most meaningful to you from this chapter, respond to one (or more) of these questions in the Journal on the following page:

- What impact does the loving way of Jesus have on your heart?
- As you and your friends love one another, how might you all be helping others see God and His love?
- What one action step are you motivated to take in response to what God has taught you?

JOURNAL

SUGGESTED MEMORY VERSE:

LOVING PEOPLE DIFFERENT FROM ME — EPHESIANS 2:14, NLT

For Christ himself has brought peace to us. He united Jews and Gentiles into one people when, in his own body on the cross, he broke down the wall of hostility that separated us.

DIGGING DEEPER

LEARNING PROJECT

Consider talking with a friend or acquaintance about your differences. Ask them how they've been stereotyped by others, and about their stereotypes of you. Jesus didn't allow the cultural stereotypes of lepers, Samaritans, or women to distance Him. Talk about what stereotypes might be hindering you from showing love to each other. (But don't expect stereotypes, yours or others, to change overnight. It's a lifelong process!)

Loving people different from you will require a "go-to" rather than a "come-to" attitude. You'll need to take little initiatives to go with your friends into another's world, not just waiting until someone comes into yours. That's what Jesus did. He came into our world with humility.

THINKING OUTSIDE MY CULTURAL BOX	LIVING AMONG THOSE DIFFERENT FROM ME
☐ Recognize that I live in a multiethnic society	☐ Become a compassion-driven person
☐ Understand the gap between my world and my neighbor's world	☐ Live authentically and attractively by the power of the Holy Spirit
☐ Develop skills to connect in relevant and sensitive ways with people	☐ Work, serve, worship, eat, learn, and play alongside others
☐ Take little initiatives to befriend and serve people —Eddie Broussard, *The Core: Environments of Grace and Truth*	☐ Keep promises and earn the trust of others ☐ Persevere with people ☐ Pray often and trust God to fulfill my desires for connecting with others

From these suggestions above, check one or two that you want to purposefully develop over the next few months — and consider doing it with others, not just alone. Describe specifically how you could begin to make it part of your life.

CHAPTER 7
RESISTING SATAN

It's been happening more and more often to Blaine. All those accusing, shaming thoughts that go through his head. Sure, he's made some mistakes with girls. But the voices inside keep telling him what a loser he is and how he'll never have what it takes to be a real man. Going to the porn sites on the Internet makes him feel better . . . until the shame starts all over again. His mother is so worried about his withdrawal from dating that she went to see an astrologer about him.

Blaine's friends bugged him to go to that video room with them again. Even though it makes him feel like one of the guys, the games they like to play creep him out — killing cops and all the blood. The video games with demons are even worse. He keeps telling himself that it's all "virtual" and only a game. But still he senses something dark and evil getting its hooks into him. He's desperate to get free from this darkness and feel clean again like he used to.

What impact do you think all the images Blaine looks at are having on his view of reality? On his soul?

We are involved in an invisible war, a cosmic conflict that has eternal implications (Ephesians 6:12). It is real, it is serious, and it is ultimate in its consequences. We are soldiers in the battle that matters most.

— CHIP INGRAM, *THE INVISIBLE WAR*

PAUSE 1_EXPLORING WHAT GOD SAYS

I am staggered by the level of naiveté that most people live with regarding evil. They don't take it seriously. They don't live as though the Story has a Villain. Not the devil prancing about in red tights, carrying a pitchfork, but the incarnation of the very worst of every enemy you've met in every other story. Dear God — the Holocaust, child prostitution, terrorist bombings, genocidal governments. What is it going to take for us to take evil seriously? Life is very confusing if you do not take into account that there is a Villain. That you, my friend, have an Enemy.

— JOHN ELDREDGE, *EPIC*

How seriously do you take evil? Or Satan? *Explain.*

There is a cosmic battle going on all over this earth, with God and His angels on one side, and Satan and his demons on the other. Satan does have influence and dominion on this earth; God also has a kingdom on this earth and in heaven. The two are in constant conflict over the souls of humans and all creation. It's a dramatic story of captives rescued and hostages ransomed. It is the real story overarching human history. The fantastic news is that in this spiritual battle, Satan ultimately loses and God wins!

KINGDOMS IN CONFLICT

As you read and mark these verses, write in the following chart whatever you observe about the conflict between the dominion of Satan and the kingdom of God.

EPHESIANS 2:1-2. As for you, you were dead in your transgressions and sins, in which you used to live when you followed the ways of this world and of the ruler of the kingdom of the air, the spirit who is now at work in those who are disobedient.

COLOSSIANS 1:12-14. Giving thanks to the Father, who has qualified you to share in the inheritance of the saints in the kingdom of light. For he has rescued us from the dominion of darkness and brought us into the kingdom of the Son he loves, in whom we have redemption, the forgiveness of sins.

1 JOHN 5:19. We know that we are children of God, and that the whole world is under the control of the evil one.

DOMINION OF SATAN	KINGDOM OF GOD
• Satan rules this dark world	

SATAN'S CORE NATURE AND AGENDA

From these passages, what is Satan's core nature?

SATAN'S NATURE

JOHN 8:44. You belong to your father, the devil, and you want to carry out your father's desire. He was a murderer from the beginning, not holding to the truth, for there is no truth in him. When he lies, he speaks his native language, for he is a liar and the father of lies.

1 PETER 5:8. Be self-controlled and alert. Your enemy the devil prowls around like a roaring lion looking for someone to devour.

Satan is the supreme Deceiver. What is one lie (or one half-truth) of Satan that you've been vulnerable to in the past or present?

The father of lies twists the truth and distorts reality. He is the author of cynicism and skepticism, mistrust and despair, sick thinking and self-hatred.

— BRENNAN MANNING, *THE RABBI'S HEARTBEAT*

CHRIST'S TRIUMPH AND SATAN'S DEFEAT

The Bible gives away the end of the story: it ends with Jesus on the throne and Satan in the pit! From these passages, find key truths about the outcome of this spiritual battle, and write them on the chart below.

> *DANIEL 2:44. In the time of those kings, the God of heaven will set up a kingdom that will never be destroyed, nor will it be left to another people. It will crush all those kingdoms and bring them to an end, but it will itself endure forever.*
>
> *MATTHEW 25:41. Then he [God] will say to those on his left, "Depart from me, you who are cursed, into the eternal fire prepared for the devil and his angels."*
>
> *JOHN 12:30-32. Then Jesus told them, ". . . The time for judging this world has come, when Satan, the ruler of this world, will be cast out. And when I am lifted up from the earth, I will draw everyone to myself."* (NLT)
>
> *COLOSSIANS 2:15. And having disarmed the powers and authorities, he [Christ] made a public spectacle of them, triumphing over them by the cross* (NIV)*. He stripped all the spiritual tyrants in the universe of their sham authority at the Cross and marched them naked through the streets.* (MSG)

CHRIST'S TRIUMPH	SATAN'S DEFEAT
• Christ's kingdom won't ever be destroyed—but will last forever	

From these passages, how did Christ overcome Satan, and how does this make you feel?

Until then, we still live in this very real world.

> *1 JOHN 5:19. We know that we are of God, and that the whole world lies in the power of the evil one.* (NASB)

Think of the various world systems such as entertainment, education, business, politics, or the military. Select one of these systems and explain how you think Satan influences it. How might this affect you personally?

PRAYER PAUSE

You may have said it a hundred times but not really noticed that spiritual warfare is right there in the Lord's Prayer.

> *MATTHEW 6:10,13. Your kingdom come, your will be done on earth as it is in heaven. . . . And lead us not into temptation, but deliver us from the evil one.*

Pause for a few minutes to talk with God about the coming of His kingdom on earth, and about Him delivering you from the evil one — whatever that might look like.

PAUSE 2_EXPLORING YOUR REALITY

In warfare it pays to "know your enemy." You can defend yourself from Satan's attacks if you understand his nature and agenda, and if you recognize his schemes and strategies.

SATAN'S STRATEGIES

True to his evil nature, Satan has several standard schemes we must be able to recognize "in order that Satan might not outwit us" (2 Corinthians 2:11). Match each passage below with a strategy Satan uses to attack us.

	SATAN'S OFFENSIVE STRATEGIES
___ MATTHEW 12:43-45	A. Tests us with suffering and persecution
___ 2 CORINTHIANS 4:4	B. Stirs up ungodly jealousy and selfish ambition among us
___ JAMES 3:14-15	C. Blinds our minds so we can't understand God's truth
___ REVELATION 2:10	D. Accuses and condemns us
___ REVELATION 12:10	E. Sends an evil spirit to harass us

What strategies do you think Satan uses to divide people, for example, along ethnic and socioeconomic lines?

BELIEVERS' WEAPONS AND DEFENSES

In addition to the name of Jesus, God has equipped us with everything we need to resist Satan and overcome evil. Consider these passages describing the weapons and protective armor God provides for us in our struggles with Satan.

Read EPHESIANS 6:10-18. Who are we fighting against (verse 12)?

On this shield list the pieces of armor that God provides (verses 14-18).

How does the Holy Spirit help you in spiritual warfare?

Read 2 CORINTHIANS 10:3-5. Explain what these spiritual weapons give us the power to do.

Is there any recurring thought of yours that you should "take captive" and "make it obedient to Christ"?

BELIEVERS' STRATEGIES

Match each reference below with two ways we can resist Satan's influence in our lives.

___ ___ HEBREWS 5:14

___ ___ JAMES 4:7

___ ___ REVELATION 12:11

A. Humble yourself and submit to God.

B. Learn to recognize the difference between right and wrong.

C. Be willing to pay any price, even death.

D. Grow in spiritual maturity with solid teaching of truth.

E. Resist the Devil.

F. Rely on the blood of Christ.

Satan is a deceiver at the core. So how can you train your senses to discern good and evil (Hebrews 5:14)?

How have you resisted Satan and submitted yourself to God (or failed to do so)? Illustrate with an example from your life.

Read 1 CORINTHIANS 10:13. How does this speak into your life today? How have you experienced the faithfulness of God in the midst of temptation?

REALITY CHECK

Satan tries to convince us that we can deal with our struggles on our own. Once we buy into this deception, we are less inclined to seek help and prayer support when we need it most. So we fail, and fail again, and fail again — and tell no one. Ashamed, we slip away altogether from fellowship with other Christians. Finally, isolated and alone, we pose no threat to the evil one's deadly devices.

— TOM EISENMAN, "OUR SOUL ENEMY," *DISCIPLESHIP JOURNAL*, MAY/JUNE 2006

PAUSE 3_COMING ALIVE TO GOD AND OTHERS

Occult: Dealing with supernatural influences, agencies, or phenomena [other than God] in order to bring them under human control.

— *AMERICAN HERITAGE COLLEGE DICTIONARY*

THE MANY FACES OF THE OCCULT

One way Satan tries to influence people is through a variety of occult activities. Many of these practices have become a normal part of our cultures and social lives. From these passages, circle any spiritual practices that God forbids. Also notice how God feels about them.

> *LEVITICUS 19:31. Do not defile yourselves by turning to mediums or to those who consult the spirits of the dead. I am the LORD your God.* (NLT)

> *DEUTERONOMY 18:9-14. When you enter the land the LORD your God is giving you, be very careful not to imitate the detestable customs of the nations living there. For example, never sacrifice your son or daughter as a burnt offering. And do not let your people practice fortune-telling, or use sorcery, or interpret omens, or engage in witchcraft, or cast spells, or function as mediums or psychics, or call forth the spirits of the dead. Anyone who does these things is detestable to the LORD. It is because the other nations have done these detestable things that the LORD your God will drive them out ahead of you. But you must be blameless before the LORD your God. The nations you are about to displace consult sorcerers and fortune-tellers, but the LORD your God forbids you to do such things.* (NLT)

How does God feel about these practices? Why do you think He feels this way?

These ancient practices take on modern forms in our world today. Choose some of the occult practices in the left column. (Check out a dictionary if you don't know what they mean.) Then list any specific examples you can think of for how they appear and are being popularized in movies, television, games, music, religion, entertainment, or culture.

OCCULT PRACTICES	MODERN FORMS
Fortune-telling & Omens	
Sorcery, Witchcraft, & Spells	
Mediums, Psychics, & Consulting the Dead	

From your list, how do the media depict evil, Satan, demons, or other spiritual beings — as harmless or horrible or beatable or attractive or something else?

From what the Bible says, how accurate are the media's images?

Have you ever practiced any of these things? If so, what do you believe God wants you to do now?

Do you know people involved deeply or on the fringes of the occult? What has been the impact of their involvement?

FOOTHOLDS

Another way that Satan influences people is by getting footholds or strongholds in their hearts that seem less "spiritual" than the occult practices mentioned above. But watch out! If you give him an inch (a foothold), he'll take a mile (a stronghold)! Add your own examples to the chart.

Love is not merely a defensive weapon. It is also powerful for taking the offensive against the devil. What power is greater than love to demolish strongholds built by the enemy? . . . If we wish to win this spiritual war, then, we must learn above all to love.

— PAUL THIGPEN, "OUR WEAPONRY," *DISCIPLESHIP JOURNAL*, MAY/JUNE 2006

FOOTHOLD	**STRONGHOLD**
EPHESIANS 4:26-27. "In your anger do not sin": Do not let the sun go down while you are still angry, and do not give the devil a foothold.	2 CORINTHIANS 10:4. The weapons we fight with are not the weapons of the world. On the contrary, they have divine power to demolish strongholds.
IF WE DABBLE in things like . . . • Pornography • •	. . . Satan will try to turn it into . . . • An addiction • •

Remember Blaine's story at the beginning of this chapter? What are some ways you can see Blaine, his mom, and his friends allowing Satan to have a foothold in their lives?

Can you illustrate from your life when you have bought into one of Satan's lies, or fallen for one of Satan's schemes, or allowed him to gain a foothold or stronghold in your life? How could you resist him next time he tries that scheme on you?

REALITY CHECK

It is important to deal with anything that has gotten even a small foothold in our lives. Allowed to grow, footholds can become obsessive struggles or spiritual strongholds. Through these strongholds, Satan seeks to destroy people. Sometimes footholds are established during a life-event when we turn from God and vow to fix life our way or even surrender to Satan's promise of immediate pleasure or power. Sometimes strongholds come from family and cultural patterns of resisting God. In spiritual warfare, we can draw upon Christ's authority and the power of the Holy Spirit to help us resist Satan's influence. And where we have allowed Satan to influence, oppress, or possess us previously, the Holy Spirit can heal our wounds and restore us.

What hope and confidence do these verses give you in your struggles with Satan?

1 JOHN 4:4. You, dear children, are from God and have overcome them, because the one who is in you is greater than the one who is in the world.

1 JOHN 5:18. We know that anyone born of God does not continue to sin; the one who was born of God keeps him safe, and the evil one cannot harm him.

Draw a picture or diagram showing the current conflict between Satan's dominion and God's kingdom.

Now include "the world" somewhere in your picture wherever you think it fits.

Then draw yourself and other followers of Christ into the picture.

Now include people who don't follow Jesus.

Who do you fight for? Who do you fight against? Be prepared to explain.

When we pray in the name of Jesus, our prayers become missiles that bombard the devil's camp. Paul declares, "At the name of Jesus every knee will bow, of those who are in heaven and on earth and under the earth." (Phil. 2:10 NASB). Those "under the earth" are the forces of hell, and the name of Jesus leaves them prostrate. . . . However weak we may be, evil spirits are no match for us when we have the name of Jesus in our mouths, because the demons know they must submit to the rule of Christ.

— PAUL THIGPEN, "OUR WEAPONRY," *DISCIPLESHIP JOURNAL*, MAY/JUNE 2006

PRAYER PAUSE

Satan will use shame and accusation to keep you isolated and in hiding over your struggles. Like a wounded soldier in battle, what you need is some help from your friends. If you are deeply struggling with the dominion of Satan and his demons, seek committed believers who will pray for you. Sometimes a counselor can help in sorting matters out. Don't go it alone. Even Jesus asked His disciples to pray for Him when He was facing His death. The demonic world will flee from believers who submit themselves to God and who resist Satan in prayer.

Spend time with God in prayer. Ask Him to reveal any areas of your life being influenced by Satan or opposed by him. Ask God to reveal how Satan got his hooks into that area in the first place. Ask Him to free you, to protect you, and to bless you in the name and the power of Jesus. Journal your prayer time.

PAUSE 4_JOURNEYING FORWARD

1 JOHN 4:10-11. This is love: not that we loved God, but that he loved us. . . . Dear friends, since God so loved us, we also ought to love one another.

Select one verse or passage that was meaningful to you this week and write it here.

We live in a world of images that deeply influence how we look at life. Choose a picture from this chapter that is meaningful or disturbing to you, and briefly explain why.

How have you experienced God this week?

Reflecting on what was most meaningful to you from this chapter, respond to one (or more) of these questions in the Journal on the following page:

- What impact does the loving way of Jesus have on your heart?
- As you and your friends love one another, how might you all be helping others see God and His love?
- What one action step are you motivated to take in response to what God has taught you?

JOURNAL

SUGGESTED MEMORY VERSE:

RESISTING SATAN — JAMES 4:7

Submit yourselves, then, to God. Resist the devil, and he will flee from you.

DIGGING DEEPER

CASE STUDIES: SATAN VS. EVE AND SATAN VS. JESUS

Study the story of Satan's success in tempting Eve, and the story about Satan's unsuccessful efforts to tempt Jesus. Try to identify several cunning strategies that Satan used in each case.

SATAN & EVE GENESIS 3:1-7	**SATAN & JESUS MATTHEW 4:5-11**
Satan's strategies against Eve:	Satan's strategies against Jesus:

Summarize one key lesson you learned from either story that will help you resist being "deceived by the serpent's cunning" or being "led astray from your sincere and pure devotion to Christ." (See 2 Corinthians 11:2-3.)

From COLOSSIANS 2:15 what was Jesus' strategy to defeat Satan?

Does it surprise you that His strategy involved dying? What other Scripture references can you find exploring the theme of victory as a result of death or dying?

CHAPTER 8
LOVING PEOPLE INTO GOD'S FAMILY

There it was again — the challenge to share his faith with his friends who didn't know Christ. But did God really need his help? Besides, he really didn't know how to begin.

Then one day at the gym, Jed was invited to join his friends David and Anna for Thanksgiving dinner. At their home Jed recognized several other people from the gym he'd never spoken to before, even though they had worked out side by side for weeks. Now here they all were eating together. Just before diving into the turkey, David and Anna each shared a couple of things they were thankful to God for. Several others, including Jed, did the same as they continued with the meal.

Later Jed asked David why he had invited so many club members over for dinner. David replied, "There are so many people looking for friendship. So Anna and I are always on the lookout for where God seems to be working. As we get to know people, we share our lives with them by opening our home, inviting them to visit our small group, and helping those who are ready to begin a relationship with God." He smiled. "We belong to 24 Hour Fitness, but Anna jokingly calls it 24 Hour Witness!"

Later that evening, Jed began to wonder . . . maybe God could use him in spite of his insecurities and inadequacies. Maybe he could be more intentional and invite a couple of guys from the gym over to watch football together . . . and maybe talk about Jesus.

Can you relate to Jed's desire and tension about sharing his belief in Jesus with his friends? How?

All people on earth are born physically into the family of man. But not all people go on to be reborn spiritually into the family of God. Billions of us remain hostages in the dominion of Satan, serving sin and self, until we are rescued by Christ. In this chapter we will explore how to build on our various relationships to attract others to Jesus and invite them into a personal relationship with Him. As we are intentional and authentic in our relationships, He invites us to "pass it forward." That's how His family grows. In this chapter you'll explore how your faith can become contagious.

PAUSE 1_EXPLORING WHAT GOD SAYS

> *A person's coming to Christ is like a chain with many links. There is the first link, middle links, and a last link. There are many influences and conversations that precede a person's decision to [trust] Christ. I know the joy of being the first link at times, a middle link usually, and occasionally the last link. God has not called me to only be the last link. He has called me to be faithful and to love all people.*
>
> — CLIFF KNETCHTLE, *GIVE ME AN ANSWER*

Recall the people who had a part in your "rescue" — someone who loved you just as you were, or whose life attracted you to Christ. Someone else whose personal testimony gave you hope that your life could be radically transformed too. Perhaps a different person explained the message of God's love and Christ's sacrifice to win your salvation and your trust. Each one was a link in the chain that drew you into God's forever family. Write their names here and take time to thank God for each of them.

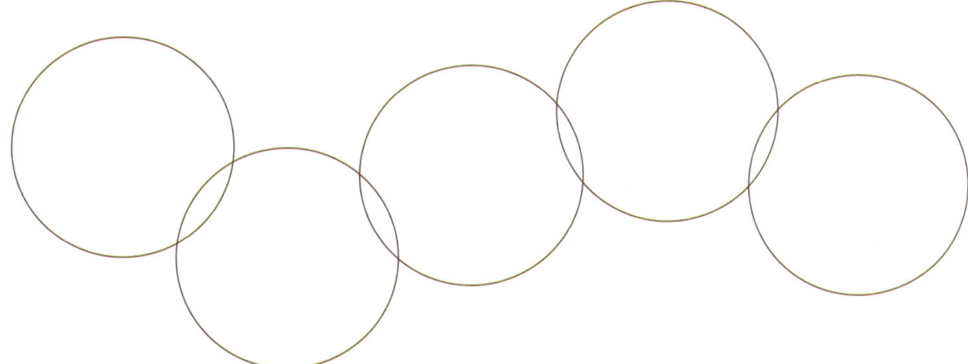

God gives you the opportunity to become a link in someone else's chain. We're all too familiar with the terrible plight of hostages. That's pretty much how the Bible describes people apart from Christ: Satan kept us captive to sin until Jesus paid the ultimate ransom. He rescued us with His blood and is bringing us home to His Father's kingdom.

Highlight or summarize in the margin whatever you notice about our condition apart from Christ.

OUR CONDITION APART FROM CHRIST

Holds us hostage

MARK 10:45. That is what the Son of Man has done: He came to serve, not to be served — and then to give away his life in exchange for many who are held hostage. (MSG)

EPHESIANS 2:1-5. Once you were dead because of your disobedience and your many sins. You used to live in sin, just like the rest of the world, obeying the devil — the commander of the powers in the unseen world. He is the spirit at work in the hearts of those who refuse to obey God. All of us used to live that way, following the passionate desires and inclinations of our sinful nature. By our very nature we were subject to God's anger, just like everyone else. But God is so rich in mercy, and he loved us so much, that even though we were dead because of our sins, he gave us life when he raised Christ from the dead. (It is only by God's grace that you have been saved!) (NLT)

COLOSSIANS 1:13-14. For he has rescued us from the kingdom of darkness and transferred us into the Kingdom of his dear Son, who purchased our freedom and forgave our sins. (NLT)

1 PETER 1:18-19. For you know that God paid a ransom to save you from the empty life you inherited from your ancestors. And the ransom he paid was not mere gold or silver. It was the precious blood of Christ, the sinless, spotless Lamb of God. (NLT)

Now go back and underline what Christ did to rescue us from our slavery. Summarize here.

Why do you think our freedom is so important to God?

What's so urgent about this? What will happen to anyone who is not "rescued . . . from the kingdom of darkness" (Colossians 1:13)?

The dominion of Satan is inhabited by slaves — slaves to sin, slaves to him. Who inhabits God's kingdom?

How does Christ continue to free us throughout our lives?

DEMONSTRATING THE GOSPEL WITH OUR LIVES

How have you seen the gospel "preached" without using words?

Preach the gospel. And if necessary, use words.

— ATTRIBUTED TO ST. FRANCIS OF ASSISI

The first way we can intentionally draw people to Christ is by the way we live. Mark whatever these verses reveal about how others can come to know God by observing our lives.

2 CORINTHIANS 2:14-16. But thanks be to God, who always leads us in triumphal procession in Christ and through us spreads everywhere the fragrance of the knowledge of him. For we are to God the aroma of Christ among those who are being saved and those who are perishing. To the one we are the smell of death; to the other, the fragrance of life. And who is equal to such a task?

1 THESSALONIANS 4:10-12. Indeed, you already show your love for all the believers throughout Macedonia. Even so, dear brothers and sisters, we urge you to love them even more. Make it your goal to live a quiet life, minding your own business and working with your hands, just as we instructed you before. Then people who are not Christians will respect the way you live, and you will not need to depend on others. (NLT)

COLOSSIANS 3:12-17. So, chosen by God for this new life of love, dress in the wardrobe God picked out for you: compassion, kindness, humility, quiet strength, discipline. Be even-tempered, content with second place, quick to forgive an offense. Forgive as quickly and completely as the Master forgave you. And regardless of what else you put on, wear love. It's your basic, all-purpose garment. Never be without it.

Let the peace of Christ keep you in tune with each other, in step with each other. None of this going off and doing your own thing. And cultivate thankfulness. Let the Word of Christ — the Message — have the run of the house. Give it plenty of room in your lives. Instruct and direct one another using good common sense. And sing, sing your hearts out to God! Let every detail in your lives — words, actions, whatever — be done in the name of the Master, Jesus, thanking God the Father every step of the way. (MSG)

From these verses, list several key things about our lives individually and in our communities of faith that will attract people to us (and to Jesus in us).

Think of the people you let in close enough to get a good "whiff" of your life. Which of these options do you think would attract them to Christ in you:

____ keeping your struggles hidden so you don't make God look bad
____ admitting your struggles so others can see Jesus working in you

Explain your answer.

PAUSE 2_EXPLORING YOUR REALITY

So, don't be afraid that you cannot answer someone's questions. If they are sincere, God will answer all the questions that that person has. You just introduce Him to that person, and share what He has done for you. No one can argue with your experience. It is not an intellectual theory. It is a true piece of history. You lived it. Share it, and share Him.

— HTTP://WWW.CLOUDTOWNSEND.COM/ARTICLES/7ARTICLES10.HTM, *COPYRIGHT 2000, CLOUD-TOWNSEND RESOURCES. ALL RIGHTS RESERVED.* HENRY CLOUD, PHD, *OVERCOMING THE FEAR FACTOR IN SHARING YOUR FAITH.*

Demonstrating the gospel with those outside God's family begins as a process of building relationships of love and trust. Then we can move beyond just relating positively and can also begin conversing our faith with others. Let's say that you and the other believers you hang out with relate to one another lovingly. How do you think this would impact the people you all live among who are still considering Jesus?

In the space below, write some effective — and some ineffective — ways of talking with others about the truth and love you are experiencing with Jesus.

What has been your experience as you've tried to tell others about Jesus' impact in your life? Looking back, is there anything you would change?

Ask God to impress on your heart the names of three specific people that you are motivated to intentionally talk with about Jesus. Write their initials here:

What should you always be prepared to do, according to this verse?

> *1 PETER 3:15. But in your hearts set apart Christ as Lord. Always be prepared to give an answer to everyone who asks you to give the reason for the hope that you have. But do this with gentleness and respect.*

What motivated you to initially respond to Jesus, and what continues to motivate you to trust Him?

Every person who has met Christ personally has a story to tell to others — even a guy who had been traumatized by a demon.

> *MARK 5:18-20. As Jesus was getting into the boat, the man who had been demon-possessed begged to go with him. Jesus did not let him, but said, "Go home to your family and tell them how much the Lord has done for you, and how he has had mercy on you." So the man went away and began to tell in the Decapolis how much Jesus had done for him. And all the people were amazed.*

What if Jesus were to ask you to "Go home to your family and tell them how much the Lord has done for you"? How prepared do you feel today to give them an answer? *Explain.*

What would you actually tell them? (Summarize in a few sentences here.)

In these passages, notice how Paul met people on their terms — not his. He adapted himself and entered their world rather than expecting people to enter his. Underline anything that illustrates his flexibility and personal sacrifice in relating to people outside God's family.

> *1 CORINTHIANS 9:19-23. Even though I am free of the demands and expectations of everyone, I have voluntarily become a servant to any and all in order to reach a wide range of people: religious, nonreligious, meticulous moralists, loose-living immoralists, the defeated, the demoralized — whoever. I didn't take on their way of life. I kept my bearings in Christ — but I entered their world and tried to experience things from their point of view. I've become just about every sort of servant there is in my attempts to lead those I meet into a God-saved life. I did all this because of the Message. I didn't just want to talk about it; I wanted to be in on it!* (MSG)

ASK YOURSELF: "How willing am I to live and adapt myself so that the people God brings around me can really hear His message from me?"

WRITE OUT A BRIEF PRAYER telling God where you are and where you would like to be in this process.

DEVELOPING YOUR STORY

In the Digging Deeper section, you'll have an opportunity to process the story of your coming to trust Christ so that you are prepared to share it when you get a chance. Plan to set aside an hour or two to prayerfully process your story of trusting Christ, and write it out. Your own testimony can be very attractive to your friends on their own spiritual journeys.

Jesus' compassion moved Him to tell the story of God's love. Our impulse to tell the salvation story arises from listening to the heartbeat of the risen Jesus within us. Telling the story does not require that we become ordained ministers or flamboyant street-corner preachers, nor does it demand that we try to convert people by concussion with one sledgehammer blow of the Bible after another. It simply means we share with others what our lives used to be like, what happened when we met Jesus, and what our lives are like now.

— BRENNAN MANNING, *THE RABBI'S HEARTBEAT*

PAUSE 3_COMING ALIVE TO GOD AND OTHERS

So what stops us from talking about Christ? Just plain old fear of rejection is enough to keep many of us from verbally sharing the truth of Jesus with others. Or fear that we won't know the answers for people's tough faith questions. Sometimes we shrink back because we know that in a lot of ways, we still struggle like everyone else. Even though we are flawed and very much in-process, we can still live the ways of Jesus and speak the truth of Jesus in love. And as we pray and genuinely follow Him, God uses us to draw others to Himself.

Read Paul's plea for Jesus' followers to tell others about "the One who can be trusted."

> *ROMANS 10:14-15. But how can people call for help if they don't know who to trust? And how can they know who to trust if they haven't heard of the One who can be trusted? And how can they hear if nobody tells them? And how is anyone going to tell them, unless someone is sent to do it? That's why Scripture exclaims, "A sight to take your breath away! Grand processions of people telling all the good things of God!"* (MSG)

As you imagine being part of the "grand processions of people telling all the good things of God," how does your heart respond to this plea? How does your will respond?

Don't assume that people already know the basic facts about Jesus — many people don't have a clue. From each passage below, identify just one or two key truths about God or Jesus that you might — over time — explain to someone as you help them understand the gospel. Summarize in the margin.

	WHAT GOD GIVES/DOES FOR US
JOHN 1:12-13. Yet to all who received him, to those who believed in his name, he gave the right to become children of God — children born not of natural descent, nor of human decision or a husband's will, but born of God.	God makes us His children & brings us into His family when we are "born" of God.

1 JOHN 1:8-9. If we claim to be without sin, we deceive ourselves and the truth is not in us. If we confess our sins, he is faithful and just and will forgive us our sins and purify us from all unrighteousness.

ROMANS 3:22-25. We are made right with God by placing our faith in Jesus Christ. And this is true for everyone who believes, no matter who we are. For everyone has sinned; we all fall short of God's glorious standard. Yet God, with undeserved kindness, declares that we are righteous. He did this through Christ Jesus when he freed us from the penalty for our sins. For God presented Jesus as the sacrifice for sin. People are made right with God when they believe that Jesus sacrificed his life, shedding his blood. (NLT)

The gospel also includes good news about what will happen to us after we trust Christ. In the margin, summarize one or two key truths from each of these passages about the life we have to look forward to in God's family.

LIFE IN GOD'S FAMILY

ROMANS 8:1,15-17. So now there is no condemnation for those who belong to Christ Jesus. . . . So you have not received a spirit that makes you fearful slaves. Instead, you received God's Spirit when he adopted you as his own children. Now we call him, "Abba, Father." For his Spirit joins with our spirit to affirm that we are God's children. And since we are his children, we are his heirs. In fact, together with Christ we are heirs of God's glory. But if we are to share his glory, we must also share his suffering. (NLT)

EPHESIANS 2:4-9. But because of his great love for us, God, who is rich in mercy, made us alive with Christ even when we were dead in transgressions — it is by grace you have been saved. And God raised us up with Christ and seated us with him in the heavenly realms in Christ Jesus, in order that in the coming ages he might show the incomparable riches of his grace, expressed in his kindness to us in Christ Jesus. For it is by grace you have been saved, through faith — and this not from yourselves, it is the gift of God — not by works, so that no one can boast.

ROMANS 5:10-11. For since our friendship with God was restored by the death of his Son while we were still his enemies, we will certainly be saved through the life of his Son. So now we can rejoice in our wonderful new relationship with God because our Lord Jesus Christ has made us friends of God. (NLT)

What does this amazing plan tell us about God's heart for us?

Look back at what you wrote in the margin above — all God has done to invite you into relationship and lavish His good gifts on you. How have you experienced this relationship and the goodness of these gifts? What are you most grateful for?

Imagine someone you know and care about asking you this question: "What is so good about Jesus that you think I should get to know Him and trust Him with my life?" How would you answer your friend? (Don't try to write this; just say it out loud.)

PRAYER PAUSE

> *COLOSSIANS 4:3-4. Also pray for us that God will give us an opportunity to tell people his message. Pray that we can preach the secret that God has made known about Christ. This is why I am in prison. Pray that I can speak in a way that will make it clear, as I should.* (NCV)

The foundation of reaching out to others in Jesus' name is prayer and the work of the Holy Spirit in their lives. Who are you praying for? And who are you praying with?

In your group, devote some time praying together for the spreading of the good news of Jesus and His kingdom to all people, including specific family members and friends within your daily routine, as well as people all over the world. Also ask Him to help you live out and converse the gospel with some of these people. Journal your prayer time.

PAUSE 4_JOURNEYING FORWARD

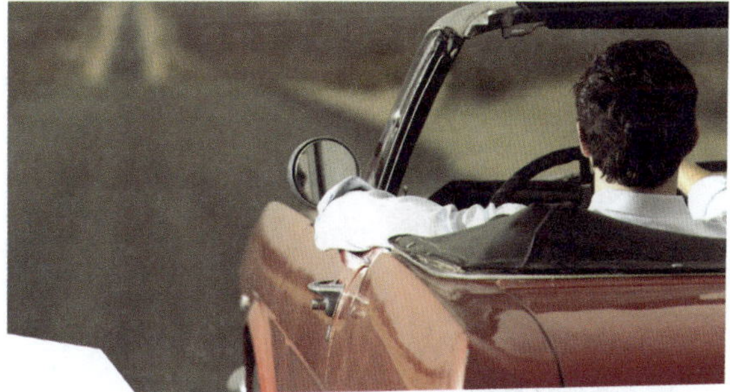

> *1 JOHN 4:10-11. This is love: not that we loved God, but that he loved us. . . . Dear friends, since God so loved us, we also ought to love one another.*

Select one verse or passage that was meaningful to you this week and write it here.

We live in a world of images that deeply influence how we look at life. Choose a picture from this chapter that is meaningful or disturbing to you, and briefly explain why.

How have you experienced God this week?

Reflecting on what was most meaningful to you from this chapter, respond to one (or more) of these questions in the Journal on the following page:

- What impact does the loving way of Jesus have on your heart?
- As you and your friends love one another, how might you all be helping others see God and His love?
- What one action step are you motivated to take in response to what God has taught you?

JOURNAL

SUGGESTED MEMORY VERSE:

SHARING MY FAITH — 1 PETER 3:15

But in your hearts set apart Christ as Lord. Always be prepared to give an answer to everyone who asks you to give the reason for the hope that you have. But do this with gentleness and respect.

DIGGING DEEPER

THE STORY OF YOUR JOURNEY WITH JESUS

This is your opportunity to write out your story of what drew you to Christ, how you responded, and the impact He has had on your life. Being able to tell your story succinctly (3-4 minutes max) is an excellent way to "prepare to give an answer" (1 Peter 3:15). Use words that someone not familiar with the Bible or church vocabulary could understand. (In other words, avoid the religious jargon.) When sharing Christ's impact on you, it's okay to mention an on-going struggle or unresolved issue. Your transformation is a lifelong process.

Depending on how complicated your story is, this will probably take you an hour or two to prepare. So try writing out a draft at a separate sitting, after you finish this chapter. Read it to someone for feedback before recording a final version in bullet or outline form below.

Are there people with whom God would like you to share your story soon?

MY LIFE BEFORE CHRIST:

(Consider: Where were you spiritually before receiving Christ and how did that affect you — your feelings, attitudes, actions, and relationships? What caused you to begin considering God/Jesus as a solution to your needs?)

WHY AND HOW I CAME TO CHRIST:

(Consider: What realization did you come to that finally motivated you to trust Christ? Specifically, how did you receive Christ? Who was involved in your journey to receive Christ?)

IMPACT ON MY LIFE AS I HAVE FOLLOWED CHRIST:

(Consider: How did your life begin changing after you trusted Christ? What new struggles have you encountered? What benefits have you experienced since becoming His follower?)

CHAPTER 9

PARTNERING WITH GOD IN HIS KINGDOM

Children with minimal educational opportunities, poor conditions, spiritual darkness — just a few of the things that burdened Kato's heart. As an agriculture professor in the U.S., he remembers vividly his Ugandan church's dream back home to build a small library in their village to expose people to the gospel through access to Bibles, other literature, and films. He and his friends back home dreamed of offering literacy training to help kids learn how to read and potentially break their hopeless cycle of poverty. If it hadn't been for a missionary couple that helped Kato get an education, he'd still be locked into that same dead-end cycle.

Then Kato met Peter at a farm-related workshop and they became friends. As they began praying together over personal and family needs, Peter's desire to help the Ugandan villagers grew until he asked Kato, "What can I do?"

Kato recruited Peter and some friends from their church to provide financial resources. The Ugandans came up with a simple plan and gave their time and the basic materials. Kato's brother back home tells how the whole village — believers, Muslims, animists, everybody — worked side-by-side making bricks for the library.

These partnerships are helping advance the gospel halfway around the world. Peter figures he doesn't have to leave the marketplace to be in the thick of the action where God is at work!

How many partnerships do you see going on in this story? List them.

What touches you most about this story?

PAUSE 1_EXPLORING WHAT GOD SAYS

We're called to live with new eyes, grace-healed eyes . . . seeing every moment, especially those moments when the sick and the sinful throng close about, as an opportunity to do good. And we're called to live with new hearts: to let the cleanness inside us spill out, washing the filth, the evil, the sickness outside us. We're to spend our heart's energy not looking for ways to enter and exit the [work]place with the least amount of involvement, touching, presence; we're to enter the [work]place looking for ways to bring God's kingdom, light, healing into it.

— MARK BUCHANAN, *YOUR GOD IS TOO SAFE*

When the triune God created all that is, it was an act of partnership between Father, Son, and Holy Spirit. And when He designed men and women in His image, He gifted us with creativity. Then He invited all people to partner with Him as stewards over His created earth and all its living creatures. From these verses, circle several tasks that God commissioned humans to do and list them in the margin.

GENESIS 1:26,28. Then God said, "Let us make man in our image, in our likeness, and let them rule over the fish of the sea and the birds of the air, over the livestock, over all the earth, and over all the creatures that move along the ground." . . . God blessed them and said to them, "Be fruitful and increase in number; fill the earth and subdue it. Rule over the fish of the sea and the birds of the air and over every living creature that moves on the ground."

GENESIS 2:15. The LORD God took the man and put him in the Garden of Eden to work it and take care of it.

TASKS FROM CREATION

1.

2.

3.

4.

5.

6.

7.

Who do you think this command from Genesis still applies to today, if anybody? How inclusive is it?

Look at some of those tasks again: rule, work, subdue, take care of. How do you see these tasks from creation relating to the everyday world of work and family life even today?

Some people think they have to leave the ordinary world of jobs and work and the marketplace, and go into something else called "ministry" in order to really work together with God. From COLOSSIANS 3:17,23-24, finish the sentence in several ways.

We are partnering with God when . . .

When you go to work every day, stay home to work, or do school work, do you have a sense of partnering with God in creating or doing something useful or meeting some need? If so, how?

Read PHILIPPIANS 2:14-16. What particular "darkness" do you think God has positioned you to bring His light into? What does (or could) that look like?

Jesus announced the presence of the Kingdom of God. . . . At the end, He accepted the title "King." . . . He clearly intended that everyone know that the rule of God was comprehensive, established over body as well as soul, over society as well as individuals, in our external behavior as well as our internal disposition, over cities and nations as well as homes and churches. . . . Salvation is God's determination to rescue His creation; it is his activity in recovering the world. It is personal and impersonal, it deals with souls and cities, it touches sin and sickness. There is a reckless indiscriminateness about salvation.

— EUGENE PETERSON, *REVERSED THUNDER*

As His body, Jesus' followers today are still called to a holistic ministry to develop and disciple people. He sends us into every segment of society, including living among the poor, the broken, the rich, and the habitually hardened, and involving the whole person — not just the spiritual side. So, in addition to partnership with God as stewards over His entire creation, God also invites His children to partner with Him by doing kind acts and loving service to others.

From these verses, finish the sentence in several ways.

EPHESIANS 2:10. *We are partnering with God when . . .*

MATTHEW 26:34-40. *We are partnering with God when . . .*

ISAIAH 58:6-7. *We are partnering with God when . . .*

Let these verses above stimulate you to imagine what part you could play along with others on a "global" scale, as well as individually on a "local" scale.

Collectively believers in the past:	Collectively believers today might:	Individually or with a few friends, I could:
• Clara Barton started the American Red Cross to serve wounded soldiers.	• Sleep outdoors overnight to raise awareness of displaced children in war-torn Uganda	• Open my home to a disaster victim
• William Wilberforce left a preaching ministry to mobilize the British to abolish slavery.	•	•
•	•	•
•	•	•
•	•	•

PAUSE 2_EXPLORING YOUR REALITY

Imagine the impact if God's people lived and worked next door to everywhere. You might be the only hands and feet of Jesus at the place you work or in your apartment building or on your sports team. You may be the only human voice God has available to speak through, or the only disciple whose shoulder He can tap to meet the needs of the people around you. You may be the only partner He can call on in a given situation.

What is one way you think God has used you to serve others, perhaps without you even recognizing it at the time?

When was one time you may have been partnering with God, simply through your loving presence, just being with someone who needed to not be alone?

As we follow Jesus the King, He actually lives in us and builds His kingdom through us. Practically, how would you most enjoy and like to partner with God in your current stage of life?

EXAMPLES	YOUR DREAMS OF PARTNERING
• Listening & empathizing with hurting people	•
• Helping build housing for disaster victims	•
• Reading the Bible with others	•
• Caring for/protecting the environment	
• Volunteering at your church's food pantry	
• Praying faithfully for your friends	
• Volunteering to tutor in the inner city	
• Writing music to reach your generation	
• Working as for Jesus in your workplace	

CASE STUDY

Maria has longed for God to use her since she started walking with Him in her early teens. Her family's faith tradition urged her to become a missionary nun — maybe in South America because she's fluent in Spanish. In a campus ministry, she caught the vision of being a disciple and making disciples. She has never wavered in her commitment to be involved in the Great Commission, discipling one person at a time. Through her church she has partnered with others reaching out to inner-city kids and the homeless. But marriage, two kids, and a part-time job have limited her available time for the forms of ministry she did in the past.

Maria comes to you, her best friend, and says, "I still want to partner with God. But I don't know what that should look like in this phase of my life. I just don't feel like I'm doing anything for God these days." She isn't asking you for advice on what to do. But she needs perspective on adjusting her partnering with God according to the realities of her life circumstances.

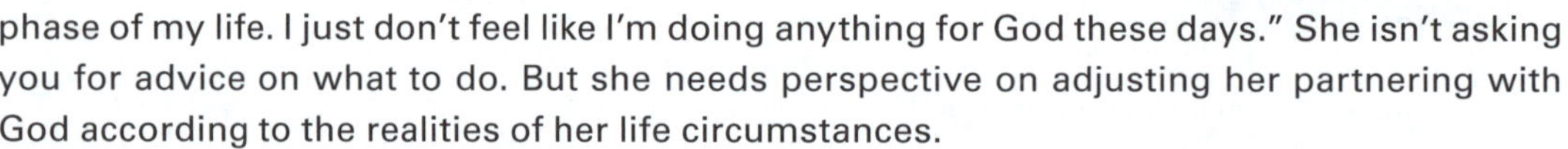

What would you talk with her about?

PAUSE 3_COMING ALIVE TO GOD AND OTHERS

Did you ever wonder what God's core passion and purpose might be? His Word tells us that, primarily, God is working actively to build His kingdom (chapter 7). And He is filling it with His family (chapter 8). Almost everything Jesus taught about who He was and what He was doing, He expressed in terms of His "message of the kingdom" (more than fifty times just in the book of Matthew).

Highlight the word "kingdom" in these verses. Then summarize below whatever you notice about God's kingdom.

LUKE 12:32. Do not be afraid, little flock, for your Father has been pleased to give you the kingdom.

MATTHEW 24:14. And this gospel of the kingdom will be preached in the whole world as a testimony to all nations, and then the end will come.

LUKE 22:28-30. You are those who have stood by me in my trials. And I confer on you a kingdom, just as my Father conferred one on me, so that you may eat and drink at my table in my kingdom and sit on thrones, judging the twelve tribes of Israel.*

**Confer: To present as a gift or an honor to someone*

Summarize in bullet points or a diagram what you observed about our part in God's kingdom after Jesus' death and ascension.

It's a huge honor just to be included in God's kingdom through your faith in Jesus. But it's an even greater honor for God to "confer" His kingdom on you. How does the privilege and responsibility of receiving this gift feel to you?

What are our kingdom tasks? From these verses, identify on the left different ways God in Christ invites us into partnership with Him (chooses, appoints, etc.). On the right, record what He calls us to do.

HOW GOD INVITES US		OUR KINGDOM TASKS
Chose us Appointed us	JOHN 15:16. You did not choose me, but I chose you and appointed you to go and bear fruit—fruit that will last. Then the Father will give you whatever you ask in my name. 2 CORINTHIANS 5:15–6:1. He died for everyone so that those who receive his new life will no longer live for themselves. Instead, they will live for Christ, who died and was raised for them. . . . [18] And all of this is a gift from God, who brought us back to himself through Christ. And God has given us this task of reconciling people to him. For God was in Christ, reconciling the world to himself, no longer counting people's sins against them. And he gave us this wonderful message of reconciliation. So we are Christ's ambassadors; God is making his appeal through us. We speak for Christ when we plead, "Come back to God!" For God made Christ, who never sinned, to be the offering for our sin, so that we could be made right with God through Christ. [6:1] As God's partners, we beg you not to accept this marvelous gift of God's kindness and then ignore it. (NLT) MARK 1:15-18. "At last the time has come!" he [John the Baptist] announced. "God's Kingdom is near! Turn from your sins and act on this glorious news!" One day as Jesus was walking along the shores of the Sea of Galilee, He saw Simon and his brother Andrew fishing with nets, for they were commercial fishermen. Jesus called out to them, "Come, follow me! And I will make you fishermen for the souls of men!" At once they left their nets and went along with him. (TLB)	To go To bear lasting fruit

Notice the different metaphors or comparisons used to describe our partnership with God: fruit-bearer, ambassador, fisherman, and so forth. As you think about partnering with God, which one do you connect with (or write your own)? Why?

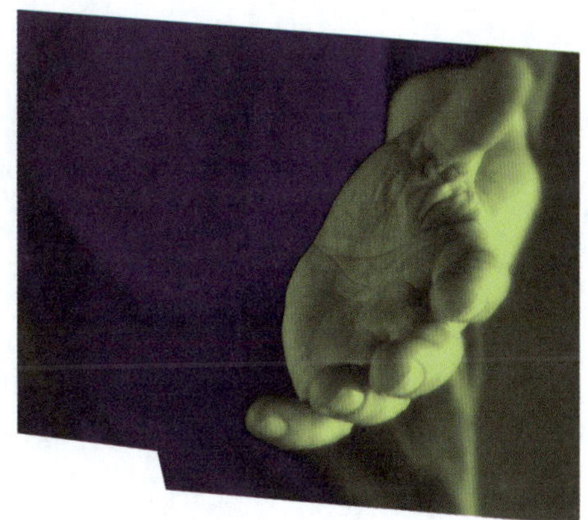

How do you respond to knowing that God has chosen you and is inviting you to partner with Him?

How does His invitation impact your personal identity or your sense of purpose and destiny?

Partnering with God in His kingdom is never a do-it-yourself project. It includes cooperating and coordinating with others — like the human body does — bringing synergy to what we do. There are different kinds of work to be done and service to be offered, so God designs us uniquely with different spiritual gifts to contribute to His kingdom.

> *1 CORINTHIANS 12:4-6. There are different kinds of gifts, but the same Spirit. There are different kinds of service, but the same Lord. There are different kinds of working, but the same God works all of them in all men.*

Which of your strengths, gifts, skills, or passions can you see God using in partnership with others to advance His kingdom? (If you're not sure, ask your friends what they see as your strengths.)

In light of your limitations and weaknesses (which we all have), how can you partner with others who are designed differently as you serve God together?

When Jesus ascended into heaven, He instructed His followers to wait in Jerusalem until the Father sent the Holy Spirit to empower them for whatever would come next (Acts 1:4). Read ACTS 1:8. Record how you think His followers might have felt to receive this commission. Also record how you feel at the thought of partnering with God nearby or far away.

What part does the Holy Spirit play in your dreams of partnering with God?

In the next chapter you will explore another way for God's children to colabor with Him — by being involved in spiritual multiplication.

FOR MORE ON SPIRITUAL GIFTS

The last two chapters of the CONNECT *study* IDENTITY: Becoming Who God Says I Am *deal with the purpose of spiritual gifts and how we can use them. Also, the assessment instrument* Breakthru: Discovering Your Spiritual Gifts *can help you identify the gifts God has given you. This inventory can be ordered through LEAD Consulting, PO Box 32026, Raleigh, NC 27622; phone 919-783-0354; www.leadconsulting-usa.com.*

PRAYER PAUSE

Take time to pray over God's invitation for you to partner with Him. Pray over questions like these, listening for the Holy Spirit's moving: Are there people far away or close by that God wants you to pray for? To help support? To help others go to? To go to yourself? Are there ways He wants you to partner in building society and stewarding nature? Also consider praying this prayer together out loud in your group:

> *O GOD, you have made of one blood all the peoples of the earth, and sent your blessed Son to preach peace to those who are far off and to those who are near: Grant that people everywhere may seek after you and find you, bring the nations into your fold, pour out your Spirit upon all flesh, and hasten the coming of your kingdom; through Jesus Christ our Lord, who lives with you and the Holy Spirit, one God, now and for ever. Amen*
>
> — For The Mission of the Church, The Book of Common Prayer[1]

[1] Collects: Contemporary, Various #16, *The Book of Common Prayer* (New Jersey: The Seabury Press, 1979), 257.

PAUSE 4_JOURNEYING FORWARD

1 JOHN 4:10-11. This is love: not that we loved God, but that he loved us. . . . Dear friends, since God so loved us, we also ought to love one another.

Select one verse or passage that was meaningful to you this week and write it here.

We live in a world of images that deeply influence how we look at life. Choose a picture from this chapter that is meaningful or disturbing to you, and briefly explain why.

How have you experienced God this week?

Reflecting on what was most meaningful to you from this chapter, respond to one (or more) of these questions in the Journal on the following page:

- What impact does the loving way of Jesus have on your heart?
- As you and your friends love one another, how might you all be helping others see God and His love?
- What one action step are you motivated to take in response to what God has taught you?

JOURNAL

SUGGESTED MEMORY VERSE:

PARTNERING WITH GOD — JOHN 15:16

You did not choose me, but I chose you and appointed you to go and bear fruit — fruit that will last. Then the Father will give you whatever you ask in my name.

DIGGING DEEPER

Partnering with God means we're listening to Him and His agenda for our lives. For some, that agenda is nearby (local outreach); for others it is in distant lands (global missions). Take this time to explore the idea of living, serving, and telling the gospel of Jesus in your neighborhood or in distant lands. Talk to others. Remember this isn't about "the glamour of going" or the "security of staying." It's about listening and partnering with God in the calling He has for our lives. Ask God what He wants for you.

Are there people far away or close by that God wants you to pray for? To help support? To help others go to? To go to yourself?

YOUR PLANNING PROCESS

It may help to try putting your plans on paper. This would be great to work on as a group or with a close and trusted friend.

PRAYER: For whom?

ARENA: What type of service are you especially interested in?

GIVING: To whom?

PREPARATION: Do I need training, education, or development to serve better?

SERVING: What extended serving opportunity might give good experience? Is there a break in your schedule when this could happen?

OTHER FACTORS: What other factors, issues, or people need to be considered as you pursue this partnership with God?

CHAPTER 10

TRUSTING GOD FOR SPIRITUAL GENERATIONS

About how many seeds are there in a typical apple?

______ Draw them.

About how many apples are there in a seed?

______ Explain.

What does this illustration suggest about the power of multiplication?

Since creation, God has wanted us to "be fruitful and multiply" (Genesis 1:22, NASB). He wasn't merely interested in increasing the human population on earth (or He wouldn't have sent the flood in Noah's wicked generation). What God longed to see was generation upon generation of men and women who love and obey Him and honor Him through their lifestyles. But where would they come from? In this chapter you will explore two pathways God has used to increase the number of God-lovers.

PAUSE 1_EXPLORING WHAT GOD SAYS

PATHWAY OF BIOLOGICAL GENERATIONS

In the pathway of biological generations, God wants to provide spiritual guidance and leadership through families. Parents and grandparents are called to partner with God by instructing, teaching, and encouraging their children and grandchildren in a life of knowing, loving, and honoring God. They become biological generations of Christ followers. Sure, our biological families are broken and imperfect in many ways. But it is still God's heart to make Himself known through family units.

In the following verses underline any commands given to the older generation. Also circle the promised results.

DEUTERONOMY 6:2-3. So that you, your children and their children after them may fear the LORD your God as long as you live by keeping all his decrees and commands that I give you, and so that you may enjoy long life. Hear, O Israel, and be careful to obey so that it may go well with you and that you may increase greatly in a land flowing with milk and honey, just as the LORD, the God of your fathers, promised you.

PSALM 78:2-8. For I will speak to you in a parable. I will teach you hidden lessons from our past — stories we have heard and known, stories our ancestors handed down to us. We will not hide these truths from our children; we will tell the next generation about the glorious deeds of the Lord, about his power and his mighty wonders. For he issued his laws to Jacob; he gave his instructions to Israel. He commanded our ancestors to teach them to their children, so the next generation might know them — even the children not yet born — and they in turn will teach their own children. So each generation should set its hope anew on God, not forgetting his glorious miracles and obeying his commands. Then they will not be like their ancestors — stubborn, rebellious, and unfaithful, refusing to give their hearts to God. (NLT)

EXODUS 20:6. [In the first of the Ten Commandments, God describes Himself as] . . . showing love to a thousand generations of those who love me and keep my commandments.

Summarize what you just picked up about the possibilities of one generation influencing the next generation.

Do you know any families who have two or more generations of Christ followers? If so, what are your impressions of these families?

What happened to the generation that followed Joshua, and why did it happen? Read JUDGES 2:7-14.

What lessons can we learn from this dark period in the history of God's people? (This pattern of following God for a while, then forsaking Him, happened many times before and after Joshua.)

PATHWAY OF SPIRITUAL GENERATIONS

Biological generations were just the beginning of God's plan to fill the earth with His children. His plan was also to spread the good news of His saving love beyond the tiny ancient nation of Israel and beyond biological families to all people at the ends of the earth. God's family is not based on genes and DNA passed from one generation to another. What God's children have in common is His Holy Spirit and all the shared spiritual blessings we have in Christ. So He also provides other people — friends, church leaders, mature believers, etc. — to serve as spiritual helpers or spiritual parents in His family, helping younger believers grow and mature.

Where do we fit in? When we partner with God to befriend another believer or seeker, help them learn to honor God, show them how to feed on God's Word, and share their struggles, we are helping to build another spiritual generation. This opens up the possibility for any of us — regardless of what families we had or didn't have — to participate in the promised blessings of having spiritual children and of influencing the next generation of disciples.

Jesus had no biological children. But He poured His life and love into His disciples, teaching them to know, trust, and obey God.

From these words of Jesus, what did He hope they would do with His message after He ascended?

JOHN 17:18-21. As you sent me into the world, I have sent them into the world. For them I sanctify myself, that they too may be truly sanctified. My prayer is not for them alone. I pray also for those who will believe in me through their message, that all of them may be one. Father, just as you are in me and I am in you. May they also be in us so that the world may believe that you have sent me.

JOHN 15:16. You did not choose me, but I chose you and appointed you to go and bear fruit — fruit that will last.

The apostle Paul also had no biological children. Yet he became the spiritual father of many.

PHILIPPIANS 2:20-22. I have no one else like him, who takes a genuine interest in your welfare. For everyone looks out for his own interests, not those of Jesus Christ. But you know that Timothy has proved himself, because as a son with his father he has served with me in the work of the gospel.

2 TIMOTHY 2:2. [Paul writing to Timothy] And the things you have heard me say in the presence of many witnesses entrust to reliable men who will also be qualified to teach others.

From 2 TIMOTHY 2:2, fill in the boxes to identify several spiritual generations.

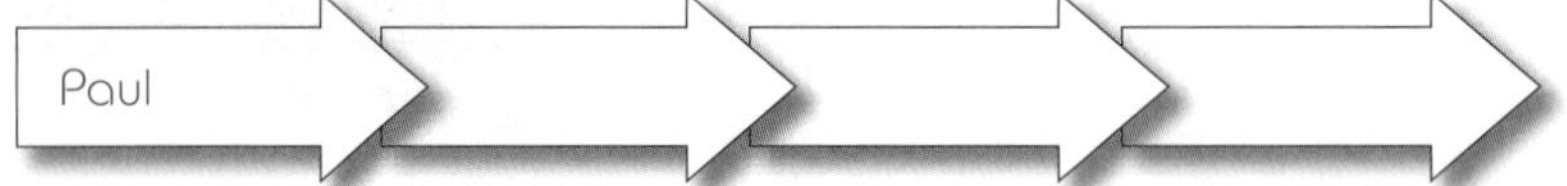

CASE STUDY: ABRAHAM

BACKGROUND

Almost 4,000 years ago, God called Abraham to move to an unknown land with his wife Sarah. Because of Abraham's faith, God chose him to become the founder of a new nation, as well as the biological and spiritual "father" of countless generations of God-lovers after him who would make God known on the earth. When Abraham was seventy-five years old (and his wife, Sarah, was way too old to get pregnant), God gave him this amazing promise.

Highlight or circle each thing God promised to do for and through Abraham and Sarah.

GENESIS 17:3-8. Abram fell facedown, and God said to him, "As for me, this is my covenant with you: You will be the father of many nations. No longer will you be called Abram; your name will be Abraham, for I have made you a father of many nations. I will make you very fruitful; I will make nations of you, and kings will come from you. I will establish my covenant as an everlasting covenant between me and you and your descendants after you for the generations to come, to be your God and the God of your descendants after you. The whole land of Canaan, where you are now an alien, I will give as an everlasting possession to you and your descendants after you; and I will be their God."

GENESIS 22:17-18. I will surely bless you and make your descendants as numerous as the stars in the sky and as the sand on the seashore. Your descendants will take possession of the cities of their enemies, and through your offspring all nations on earth will be blessed, because you have obeyed me. [The word "offspring" is singular, and can also be translated "seed."]

Who was this "offspring" of Abraham through whom "all nations on earth will be blessed"? (See Galatians 3:16.)

What did God expect Abraham to do in response to these marvelous promises? (See Genesis 18:18-19.)

How do you think Abraham (and Sarah) responded to such a blessing?

Abraham believed God for biological and spiritual generations, simply because He trusted God to keep His promise. He didn't live to see his grandson Jacob, nor his other biological descendants many generations later — King David and Jesus. Another exciting part of God fulfilling His promise to Abraham is identifying some of Abraham's spiritual descendants. Read Galatians 3:29 and fill in the last arrow below.

REFLECTION

The next time you gaze at the stars in the sky or walk on the seashore (see Genesis 22:17), think about God's promise to Abraham — that one of those stars or grains of sand represents you. As an heir to the same promise, are you trusting God for generations to come from your life, too? If you have never thought about this before, stop for a time of prayer.

It now becomes apparent that God never was thinking merely about physical generations in his instructions to Israel. He intended a convergence of physical generations with the spiritual right from the beginning. God had this generation of ours in mind when he gave Abraham his promise. We, too, are children of Abraham, and, as such, have rights to those same promises!

— JIM PETERSEN & MIKE SHAMY, *THE INSIDER*

PAUSE 2_EXPLORING YOUR REALITY

So what is your role in this grand plan for God to reveal Himself to the nations? Are you, too, called to be a spiritual parent or influencer to someone else? Explore these two ways you can partner with God in spiritual multiplication.

PATHWAY 1:
PARTNERING WITH GOD THROUGH FAMILIES / BIOLOGICAL GENERATIONS

God wants our offspring to be godly. This is his first line of approach in discipling the nations. It is the primary avenue to spiritual generations. So he instructs us in how to go about this. He says, "Make my ways your topic of conversation as you sit, as you walk, as you lie down, and as you get up." We are always in one of those four positions.

— JIM PETERSEN & MIKE SHAMY, *THE INSIDER*

Consider this counsel for parents given by Moses.

> *DEUTERONOMY 6:5-9. Love the LORD your God with all your heart and with all your soul and with all your strength. These commandments that I give you today are to be upon your hearts. Impress them on your children. Talk about them when you sit at home and when you walk along the road, when you lie down and when you get up. Tie them as symbols on your hands and bind them on your foreheads. Write them on the doorframes of your houses and on your gates.*

From the passage above, describe in your own words how God wants parents to pass on His Word and His ways to their children.

Who in your biological family (if anyone) has had a significant positive influence on your spiritual life? How?

Do you have children, or want to have children someday? If so, what hope or desire do you have about the influence your faith and parenting could have on future generations?

What about your brothers, sisters, or cousins? How could you begin to influence them for Christ?

PATHWAY 2: PARTNERING WITH GOD THROUGH SPIRITUAL GENERATIONS

Meditate on these verses about things that seem impossible.

> *ISAIAH 54:1-3. "Sing, O barren woman, you who never bore a child; burst into song, shout for joy, you who were never in labor; because more are the children of the desolate woman than of her who has a husband," says the LORD. "Enlarge the place of your tent, stretch your tent curtains wide, do not hold back; lengthen your cords, strengthen your stakes. For you will spread out to the right and to the left; your descendants will dispossess nations and settle in their desolate cities."*
>
> *ISAIAH 60:21-22. "Then will all your people be righteous and they will possess the land forever. They are the shoot I have planted, the work of my hands, for the display of my splendor. The least of you will become a thousand, the smallest a mighty nation. I am the LORD; in its time I will do this swiftly."*

How do these verses give hope to everyone — especially those who feel insignificant or who are childless for any reason?

What do these verses reveal about the power of spiritual multiplication?

In the passage below (often called "The Great Commission") Jesus commands us to "make disciples . . . [by] teaching them to obey everything" He commanded.

> *MATTHEW 28:18-20. Then Jesus came to them and said, "All authority in heaven and on earth has been given to me. Therefore go and make disciples of all nations, baptizing them in the name of the Father and of the Son and of the Holy Spirit, and teaching them to obey everything I have commanded you. And surely I am with you always, to the very end of the age."*

As you think about the life of Jesus, what specific things did He do in discipling His followers? Fill in the chart with things that Jesus helped His disciples . . .

. . . KNOW	. . . BELIEVE OR TRUST
• What life in His kingdom is like	• The promise of eternal life
. . . BE	**. . . DO**
• Humble servants to others	• How to talk with God and listen to Him in prayer

- Now go back to your list and write the initials of someone who has helped you in any of these activities.
- Read your list one more time and write the initials of someone you have helped in any of these things.
- Share these ideas with your small group and add ideas to your list from others in your group.

What is one difference between encouraging others to decide to follow Christ and discipling them?

Who are you "fishing" for, and who are you intentionally helping to grow as a disciple? Who could you "fish" for or help?

MATTHEW 4:19. "Come, follow me," Jesus said, "and I will make you fishers of men."

Which of your friends share this vision and are trusting God with you as you help others grow?

PRAYER PAUSE

Take a minute and pray for your family now, your future family, children, grandchildren, nieces, nephews. Ask God to bless your generations and make Himself known throughout your family line. Thank Him that it gives Him great joy to bless your family and reward your faith.

Also pray for your friends, neighbors, coworkers. Who can you come alongside to help him or her know God in a deeper way? What desires do you have to influence generations in their spiritual lives? What legacy do you want to leave through generations of Christ followers? Talk over these questions with God.

PAUSE 3_COMING ALIVE TO GOD AND OTHERS

God is not looking for brilliant men [and women], is not depending upon eloquent men, is not shut up to the use of talented men in sending His gospel out in the world. God is looking for broken men who have judged themselves in the light of the cross of Christ. When He wants anything done, He takes up men who have come to the end of themselves, whose confidence is not in themselves, but in God.

— H. A. IRONSIDE

Perhaps you're wondering if and how God could work through you. How adequate do you feel raising children to follow Him, or helping someone else mature spiritually? Consider these verses:

> *2 CORINTHIANS 4:7. But we have this treasure in jars of clay to show that this all-surpassing power is from God and not from us.*
>
> *2 CORINTHIANS 12:9. My grace is sufficient for you, for my power is made perfect in weakness.*

As you think about influencing future generations, do you feel anxious or inadequate or some other feeling? *Explain.*

How might God actually work through your weaknesses and failures — not in spite of them? How does your heart respond to God's power being made perfect in your weaknesses, especially as you influence others for Christ?

REALITY CHECK

God often described Himself in the Old Testament as the God of Abraham, Isaac, and Jacob (see Exodus 3:15). Generations were so important to Him that He named Himself after three of them. Yet, Abraham, Isaac, and Jacob were faith-filled people with real life struggles, failures, and family issues. God chose to bless them and reveal Himself in spite of their weaknesses — and even through them.

God is faithful to fulfill all His promises to us. How does this assurance give you hope to influence future generations in spite of struggles and failures — yours, your family members', and people who have influenced you spiritually?

Paul loved the believers in Thessalonica as though they were his own children. Read 1 THESSALONIANS 2:7-12, where Paul describes how he served as a biblical spiritual parent. List any qualities and actions of a good spiritual parent mentioned in this passage.

From your list, which two or three qualities/actions do you especially want to characterize you as you influence others for Jesus?

Paul compared his discipling ministry to the work of a builder — laying a foundation and then building the house with quality materials. Read 1 CORINTHIANS 3:10-15.

Who has been involved in laying a biblical spiritual foundation in your life?

Whose foundation are you helping to build?

What do you want to be rewarded for in heaven?

What in particular do you know you need to rely on the Holy Spirit for as you help others grow spiritually?

How does your church or community of believers provide this kind of help to young believers?

What if . . . tomorrow you lead someone to trust in Jesus? Would you know how to get them started in walking with Him? Would you know how to keep them going? *Explain*.

REALITY CHECK

If you answered "no" to the last question, that's okay. Consider asking your small group leader or another mature believer about how you can learn to disciple others. Explore other resources that could motivate and equip you in spiritual multiplication, such as books or workshops or training opportunities. Also consider the Digging Deeper section in this chapter. Would you ever consider coleading a group through the CONNECT series or some other form of exploring the Bible together? What might be obstacles and opportunities for you to start such a group?

Pursuing a divine vision is really an act of worship. It is a declaration of our confidence in God. It is a proclamation of how important we believe His agenda to be. And God is honored.

—ANDY STANLEY, *VISIONEERING*

How does your heart respond to the opportunity to participate in God's divine vision for the world?

What would it look like (or does it already look like) for you to "plant seeds" or "lay foundations" where you are right now? Who else are the workers alongside you?

CLOSING REFLECTION

We plant seeds that one day will grow.
We water seeds already planted knowing that they hold promise.
We lay foundations that will need further development.
We provide yeast that produces effects far beyond our capabilities.

We cannot do everything, and there is a sense of liberation in realizing that.
This enables us to do something, and to do it very well.
It may be incomplete, but it is a beginning, a step along the way, an opportunity for the Lord's grace to enter and do the rest.
We may never see the end results, but that is the difference between the master builder and the worker.

We are workers, not master builders; ministers, not messiahs.
We are prophets of a future not our own.

— Former Archbishop Oscar Romero of El Salvador

PRAYER PAUSE

As you pray, ask God how He wants to use you in the process of spiritual multiplication. Listen to Him calling you to partner with Him through generations, serving Him close to home or in far away places. In the Old Testament, God described Himself as the God of Abraham, Isaac, and Jacob. Today He might describe Himself as the God of

____ (your spiritual parents/disciplers),

_________________ (you), and ____ (your spiritual children).

Ask God to cultivate the seeds of faith you plant and give you more names to add to these blanks in years to come. Consider writing out a prayer in response to God that expresses your heart's desire for spiritual generations.

YOUR PRAYER . . .

PAUSE 4_JOURNEYING FORWARD

1 JOHN 4:10-11. This is love: not that we loved God, but that he loved us. . . . Dear friends, since God so loved us, we also ought to love one another.

Select one verse or passage that was meaningful to you this week and write it here.

We live in a world of images that deeply influence how we look at life. Choose a picture from this chapter that is meaningful or disturbing to you, and briefly explain why.

How have you experienced God this week?

Reflecting on what was most meaningful to you from this chapter, respond to one (or more) of these questions in the Journal on the following page:

- What impact does the loving way of Jesus have on your heart?
- As you and your friends love one another, how might you all be helping others see God and His love?
- What one action step are you motivated to take in response to what God has taught you?

JOURNAL

SUGGESTED MEMORY VERSE:

TRUSTING GOD FOR GENERATIONS — MATTHEW 28:18-20

Then Jesus came to them and said, "All authority in heaven and on earth has been given to me. Therefore go and make disciples of all nations, baptizing them in the name of the Father and of the Son and of the Holy Spirit, and teaching them to obey everything I have commanded you. And surely I am with you always, to the very end of the age.

DIGGING DEEPER

New spiritual life and spiritual multiplication are definitely miracles that God promises to do. We cannot dictate these blessings any more than Abraham and Sarah could produce the child of promise. But what God has promised, He will do! Our role is to walk by faith, to obey God's leading, and to claim His promise to multiply us spiritually. Some will see much spiritual fruit in their lifetime and others may only see one "Isaac." Abraham believed God's promise of a great nation even when his eyes saw only one son through Sarah. As we faithfully participate in the process, God does the miracle of spiritual multiplication.

Here are a few ideas for participating with Him at the initial phase of introducing people to Christ (evangelizing). As you read, take it to the next level by writing your own ideas for the ongoing phase of deepening people in Christ (discipling).

INITIAL EVANGELIZING APPLICATIONS	ONGOING DISCIPLING APPLICATIONS
Praying. Ask God to work in the lives of specific people. Pray for their spiritual life and journeys. By faith claim the promise that God will use you in the lives of others for the glory of God. Rely on the Holy Spirit of God for the miracle of spiritual generations.	Praying
Initiating. Ask God for discernment and boldness in initiating spiritual conversations. Sometimes we hold back and wait for others to bring up the subject. Or we may force a conversation that seems to fall flat. Step out and be real. Enjoy talking about your spiritual journey with others. And when things fall flat, don't let that stop you from initiating.	Initiating
Serving your neighbor. Jesus' way of ministering to others is a way of love. Simply serving people is a wonderful way of communicating love without words. In time these acts of kindness and service can create opportunities to speak more directly about your faith. Serving sometimes involves sacrifice. Loving sacrifice often speaks deeply to other people about the love God has placed in your heart for them.	Serving your neighbor
Listening for needs and open nerves. As we dialogue with people, their needs and desires surface. Sometimes you can ask questions. Sometimes you simply listen. And sometimes you can share from your spiritual journey and truths you have learned from the Bible and experienced in your spiritual journey.	Listening for needs and open nerves
Teaming up and including others. Spiritual multiplication occurs within the body of Christ. No one person can do it all. Introduce other believers to your friends and family who don't yet know Jesus. Let the community of believers who love one another impact them.	Teaming up and including others

Exploring the Scriptures. Many people are open to read books together and discuss what they've read. Sometimes this occurs over coffee or in a dorm room or over the Internet. Be creative. There are many good resources that can help facilitate your time in the Bible and discussion. Also discussing passages from the Bible in the context of living life is a powerful way to experience God's presence and wisdom for life.	Exploring the Scriptures
Exploring life together. The news of the kingdom of God is all around us—through symbols in nature, through the arts and sciences, through life's hardships and pleasures. As you live and explore life with others, take life experiences and relate them to your spiritual journey. Most movies have themes and longings that can be related to our spiritual journey. Major events of life (such as births, marriages, sicknesses, and deaths) are part of the spiritual mosaic that God is designing in our hearts. The beauty around us points toward God whose glory is excellent beauty. Our work relates to God's calling for humanity to be creative, to build ethical societies that worship Him, and to rule in nature while caring for it. As you minister to others, ask God to help you weave these spiritual discussions into the ordinary and major events of life.	Exploring life together
Encouraging others to decide. Following Jesus involves making decisions. Encourage others to make the initial step to follow Jesus and to continue to follow Him daily. Making these commitments will solidify and guide our spiritual journeys.	Encouraging others to decide
Loving others with truth. Ministry to others is always an act of love. This love comes from God and spreads through us to others. As you influence others continue to ask God for His love that speaks His truth in ways that demonstrate and bring life to others.	Loving others with truth
Always love God first. Sometimes we're tempted to substitute the blessings of serving God for intimacy with God Himself. As our Bridegroom, Jesus calls us first to Himself—and only then to ministry.	Always love God first
Others?	Others?

CELEBRATING YOUR GROUP

Somewhere deep down, we know that if we are to survive we must come together and rediscover ways to connect with each other, and with the earth that supports our collective life. We are social beings who need one another not just for physical survival but also for spiritual sustenance as we journey together. So our individuality only makes sense in the context of community, where we are free to become ourselves.

— JONATHAN S. CAMPBELL WITH JENNIFER CAMPBELL, *THE WAY OF JESUS*

As you and your group finish this study, it's a good time to celebrate together. Your relationships have deepened through these past weeks. You've learned much from each other — truths, joys, pains. So we encourage you to plan a celebration. Take some time to "Reflect Back," "Envision Forward," and "Pause to Affirm and Pray."

REFLECT BACK

Share how you've benefited from studying God's Word with this group of fellow spiritual journeyers.

How has your walk with God been affected?

How has your daily lifestyle changed?

What emotions surface as you reflect on your times together?

ENVISION FORWARD

What are your spiritual needs as you consider the next phase of your journey?

In what environment might these needs be met?

What continuing relationships will you have with the people in this group (casual friendship to in-depth involvement)?

Are there other people you know who could benefit from studying this series?

Would one or more people from this group facilitate a new group? Is God leading anyone to be a part of a new group?

PAUSE TO AFFIRM

Do you want to express a thank you or affirmation to anyone in the group who has influenced your life? Take time to do that.

PAUSE TO PRAY

Spend time together praying. Thank God for this part of your journey. Praise Him for who He is. Linger longer together.

WHY MEMORIZE SCRIPTURE?

You won't find the word *memorize* in the Bible. But the concept is there both in command and in example ("treasure . . . store up . . . hide" God's words in our hearts). We are encouraged to "study . . . reflect on . . . delight in . . . not forget" God's words (Psalm 119:9-16, NLT; 37:31).

- "lay hold of . . . pay attention . . . listen closely . . . keep [God's words] within your heart" (Proverbs 4:4,20-22).
- "bind them [my commands] around your neck . . . write them on the tablet of your heart" (Proverbs 3:3).
- "always treasure my commands. . . . Guard my instructions as you guard your own eyes. Tie them on your fingers as a reminder. . . . Write them on the tablet of your heart" (Proverbs 7:1-3, NLT, NIV).
- "it is good to keep these sayings in your heart" (Proverbs 22:18, NLT).
- "meditate on [God's words] day and night" (Joshua 1:8).

These same verses also explain the reasons for and benefits of memorizing Scripture:

- "that I might not sin against you . . . [my] feet do not slip" (Psalm 119:9-16; 37:31).
- "they bring life . . . and healing to their whole body" (Proverbs 4:22, NLT).
- "find favor with both God and people . . . earn a good reputation" (Proverbs 3:3-4, NLT).
- "you will trust in the Lord" (Proverbs 22:18-19, NLT).
- "you will be sure to obey everything written in it. Only then will you prosper and succeed" (Joshua 1:8, NLT).
- so that you'll "have all of them ready on your lips" (Proverbs 22:18).
- "your words . . . were my joy and my heart's delight" (Jeremiah 15:16).

Perhaps even more compelling than these reasons is seeing how powerfully God can use a person who has taken the time and effort to consistently memorize Scripture. When Jesus faced Satan (see Matthew 4:1-11), He drew from the many verses of Scripture that He had memorized in His youth to pinpoint Satan's deception and resist temptation. Where would we be if Jesus had not memorized Scripture? When Peter addressed the huge crowd on the day of Pentecost, he was given no time to consult his concordance and prepare a message! Because he had made Scripture memory a priority in his life, he could quote from three different Old Testament passages that helped bring 3,000 people to the Lord!

If you long to equip yourself to counteract Satan, resist sin, trust and obey God, listen to God's voice, and minister to others, there is no better investment of your time than memorizing Scripture.

A good place to begin is by revisiting the verses you memorized here in this study. Carry the verses around. Put them on your PDA. Put them on your computer. Review them out loud. Often. Write them out until you can say them accurately. Meditate on them. Pray over them. Tell a friend what they mean to you. Put yourself to sleep at night thinking about them. And look forward to listening to God speak to you!

I am amazed at the countless times God pulled from my mind a memorized verse that has been exactly the right thing at the right time! At times it was a comfort, at times guidance. A push ahead or a pull to stop. A reminder of His promise, a prompting for wisdom. A word for counseling another, an insight for those seeking our Lord.

— DENNIS STOKES

SCRIPTURE MEMORY VERSES

RECEIVING LOVE TO GIVE LOVE *MATTHEW 22:39* *And the second is like it: "Love your neighbor as yourself."*	*LOVING ONE ANOTHER* *JOHN 13:34-35* *A new command I give you: Love one another. As I have loved you, so you must love one another. By this all men will know that you are my disciples, if you love one another.*
FORGIVING EACH OTHER *EPHESIANS 4:32, NLT* *Instead, be kind to each other, tenderhearted, forgiving one another, just as God through Christ has forgiven you.*	*LOVING IN FAMILIES* *PSALM 68:5-6, NLT* *Father to the fatherless, defender of widows — this is God, whose dwelling is holy. God places the lonely in families.*
LOVING FRIENDS *PROVERBS 18:24, NLT* *There are "friends" who destroy each other, but a real friend sticks closer than a brother.*	*LOVING PEOPLE DIFFERENT FROM ME* *EPHESIANS 2:14, NLT* *For Christ himself has brought peace to us. He united Jews and Gentiles into one people when, in his own body on the cross, he broke down the wall of hostility that separated us.*
RESISTING SATAN *JAMES 4:7* *Submit yourselves, then, to God. Resist the devil, and he will flee from you.*	*SHARING MY FAITH* *1 PETER 3:15* *But in your hearts set apart Christ as Lord. Always be prepared to give an answer to everyone who asks you to give the reason for the hope that you have. But do this with gentleness and respect.*
PARTNERING WITH GOD *JOHN 15:16* *You did not choose me, but I chose you and appointed you to go and bear fruit — fruit that will last. Then the Father will give you whatever you ask in my name.*	*TRUSTING GOD FOR GENERATIONS* *MATTHEW 28:19-20* *Therefore go and make disciples of all nations, baptizing them in the name of the Father and of the Son and of the Holy Spirit, and teaching them to obey everything I have commanded you. And surely I am with you always, to the very end of the age.*

CONNECT SERIES OVERVIEW

CONNECT is designed to help you discover and embrace the truth Jesus spoke of in a holistic way. We long to see you enjoying life as a member of God's kingdom and family, deeply experiencing His presence, knowing His truth, resting in His love, and confident in His hope. These studies are designed to be used in small groups where people can encourage, trust, and support each other on their spiritual journeys.

CONNECT is arranged as a series of studies. These studies will present foundational biblical principles for primary relationships in life. Jesus summed up what life is all about when He said, "'Love the Lord your God with all your heart and with all your soul and with all your mind.' This is the first and greatest commandment. And the second is like it: 'Love your neighbor as yourself'" (Matthew 22:37-39). Growing in your love for God, for others, and for yourself while managing your personal life in ways that honor Him — now that is a real spiritual journey!

In case this is your first experience in the CONNECT series — or even if you have journeyed through other studies before you picked up this one — this overview may help you connect some dots.

GOD: Connecting with His Outrageous Love is about receiving God's love and loving Him in response.

IDENTITY: Becoming Who God Says I Am and *SOUL: Embracing My Sexuality and Emotions* are about discovering who God says we are and learning to live out of that true identity.

RELATIONSHIPS: Bringing Jesus into My World is about loving people — all kinds of people. Because if we're loving God and ourselves, then loving people will happen naturally.

LIFE: Thriving in a Complex World is about living life well with Jesus. You'll see these themes unfold if you study them in order. But they may also be studied individually or in any order.

Our prayer is that we all will grow in deeper intimacy with God from a heart of worship as we humbly follow Jesus' ways, truth, and life!

ABOUT THE AUTHORS

RALPH ENNIS is the Director of Intercultural Training and Development for The Navigators. Ralph and his wife, Jennifer, have ministered with The Navigators since 1975 in a variety of areas, including at Norfolk military bases, Princeton University, Richmond Community, Glen Eyrie Leadership Development Institute, and with The CoMission in Moscow, Russia. Ralph has a Master's degree in Intercultural Relations. Some of his publications include *Searching the Ordinary for Meaning; Breakthru: Discover Your Spiritual Gifts and Primary Roles; Successfit: Decision Making Preferences; An Introduction to the Russian Soul;* and *The Issue of Shame in Reaching People for Christ.*

Ralph and Jennifer currently live in Raleigh, North Carolina. They have four married children and nine grandchildren.

JUDY GOMOLL is Director of School Agreements as a National Training Team Associate. Before joining The Navigators, Judy was an educator with a specialty in curriculum development. Judy and her husband, George, served with The Navigators as missionaries in Uganda and Kenya for fifteen years, where they helped pioneer ministries in communities, churches, and at Makerere University. Judy led in leader training and designing of contextualized discipleship materials and methods. In her current role with the National Training Team, Judy is assisting in the research, development, and field testing of spiritual transformation training tools and resources. She also directs our partnerships agreements with seminaries and graduate schools.

Judy has an MA in Curriculum and Instruction, and an MA in Organizational Leadership. She and George live in Parker, Colorado.

DENNIS STOKES has been serving with The Navigators since 1973. During that time he has ministered on collegiate staff, as well as being a collegiate trainer and national training consultant. Dennis has designed, developed, and led seven summer training programs for The Navigators, and was the training coordinator for the CoMission project to the former Soviet Union. He is ordained and speaks at training events, conferences, and in church pulpits in the U.S. and twelve different countries. He also leads and participates on numerous training teams. In his role as the National Training Director for the U.S. Navigators, Dennis leads out in strategic planning, leading, and implementing national initiatives for staff training and development.

Dennis and his wife, Ellen, live in Erie, Colorado, and have three children — Christopher, Cheryl, and Amy.

CHRISTINE WEDDLE is Associate Director of National Training and Staff Development and has been on staff with The Navigators since 1997. She first connected with The Navigators when she joined the CoMission Training Team. In this role she assisted in the planning and organization of staff training events in the U.S., Russia, and the Ukraine.

Since moving to Colorado Springs in 1998, she has directed numerous national training and staff development events. She specializes in developing adult learning environments and visual resources.

REBECCA GOLDSTONE is a National Training Team consultant for The Navigators. Before joining The Navigators, Rebecca was a consulting partner with The Navigators in training and developing The CoMission project staff and leaders from the former Soviet countries. After leaving The CoMission Rebecca pioneered and developed a crosscultural urban ministry in Santa Ana, California. She is a training consultant, life coach, and serves on the faculty of Hope International University. Her role on the National Training Team consists of creating and editing resources related to spiritual transformation and strategic tools to equip leaders ministering to the millennial generation.

Rebecca and her husband, Marc, live in Irvine, California. They have two children, Ryan and Joshua.

Connect Even More!

The CONNECT series is designed to help you discover and embrace the truth Jesus spoke of in a holistic way. By using the series in a small group, you will find encouragement, trust, and support from others as you travel together on this spiritual journey.

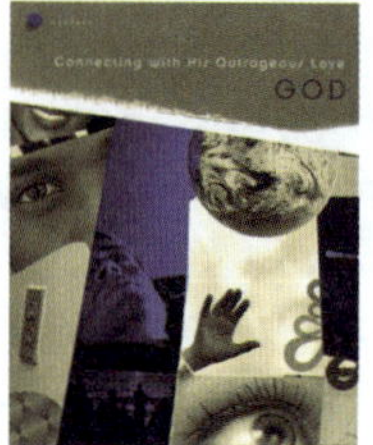

God: Connecting with His Outrageous Love

Ralph Ennis, Judy Gomoll, Dennis Stokes, Christine Weddle
978-1-60006-258-2
1-60006-258-X

This study presents a foundational biblical principle for primary relationships in life: receiving God's love and loving Him in response.

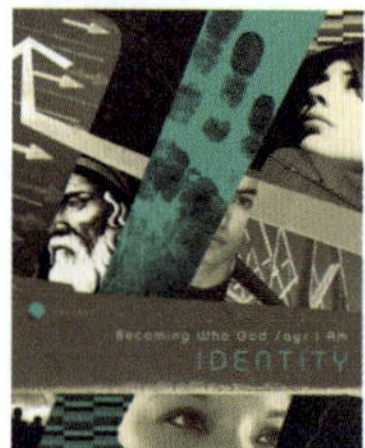

Identity: Becoming Who God Says I Am

Ralph Ennis, Judy Gomoll, Dennis Stokes, Christine Weddle
978-1-60006-259-9
1-60006-259-8

Discover who God says you are and learn to live out your true identity by loving God, others, and yourself.

Soul: Embracing My Sexuality and Emotions

Ralph Ennis, Judy Gomoll, Rebecca Goldstone, Dennis Stokes, Christine Weddle
978-1-60006-262-9
1-60006-262-8

Find out how growing in your love for God, for others, and for yourself will help manage your personal life in ways that honor Him.

Life: Thriving in a Complex World

Ralph Ennis, Judy Gomoll, Rebecca Goldstone, Dennis Stokes, Christine Weddle
978-1-60006-260-5
1-60006-260-1

Explore important areas—time, money, decisions, commitment—that play a role in living life well with Jesus.

To order copies, call NavPress at 1-800-366-7788, or log on to www.navpress.com.